# Cooking in Russia

## YouTube Channel

## Companion Reader

# VOLUME 2

by

Greg Easter

A good chef will make sure that you enjoy the first bite of a dish.

A great chef will make sure that you enjoy every bite.

A master chef will make you cry if a bite lands on the floor.

# TABLE OF CONTENTS

# INTRODUCTION

As with the first volume, this was written primarily to provide additional information for the video recipes online at:

www.youtube.com/user/cookinginrussia

## Further Explanation of the Purpose

In the first volume of this series I explained what originally motivated me to produce these videos was seeing just how much bad information was flooding YouTube, as well as the inept self-destruction of the Food Network as it shifted from culinary education to vacuous food-related entertainment. However, rather than merely trying to provide some professional and accurate cooking information, I also want to share my discovery of exotic flavors that are largely unknown, even to other chefs. The well-traveled roads of mainstream cuisines have few surprises left for serious foodies over the age of about 25. By then you know how great a marinara sauce can be when made with ripe San Marzano tomatoes and how succulent a Wagyu steak is when it is cooked and seasoned to perfection. Yawn. But there are the keys to flavors contained in this book (and the associated videos) that you don't know—no matter who you are. I don't mean things that are weird-for-the-sake-of-weird, either. I'm not talking about 48-hour braised tree bark with pickled seaweed and an enoki-caramel sauce (an actual dish I was once served). That sort of Dali-esque offering is the work of a chef who is *so* desperate to stand out and come up with something new that they forgot that food is supposed to be delicious. By the way, don't believe everything you see on television shows like MasterChef when judges are served bizarre concoctions and seem to enjoy them. Food industry publications (outside of the mainstream media) report how many of the dishes that they pretended to like on the show were absolutely terrible in reality.

At the opposite end of this extreme, we have the chef who sings the praises of how simple and uncomplicated food is the best.

Given a choice between enoki mushrooms in caramel sauce and a plate of buttered noodles, I guess I would agree that the pasta is the winner, but by no means does that imply that plain spaghetti is a culinary achievement. No offense intended to my Italian friends. The point is that simple is *only* the best if compared with something worse. In the land of television entertainment, this big lie about simplicity has been firmly implanted in the minds of viewers and even chefs and restaurateurs alike. It is absolutely not true. Look at some of the most delicious foods in the world and you'll see long lists of ingredients and complex cooking schemes to coax subtle nuances of flavor out that you would never experience otherwise.

## The Illusion of Stirring

Speaking of television cooks, and even in my own cooking videos, one can get the impression that pots are almost constantly being stirred. This is because I only record the video when there is something going on. You don't see the long stretches where food sits undisturbed, sizzling away. In fact, one of the reasons why restaurant food often has richer flavor is because cooks are busy with many things going on at the same time, so they can't stand there stirring. This lets food brown better. One of the most common mistakes home cooks make is too much stirring. Think of your bare feet on a hot road. If you keep jumping around they stay cooler. That's not how to cook feet...I mean food. ☺

## Modular Thinking of an Experienced Chef

Home cooks think in terms of meals. Seasoned professionals think in terms of components, or modules. We are not simply combining chicken and a sauce on a plate. We are combining complex preparations to make that chicken and multiple plating elements. Not only is this difficult to show in a video because the video would be very long, but even if I ignored that, it still suffers from the same problem—I would be showing you a specific recipe from start to finish, rather than imparting an understanding of the flavors and processes involved. This approach is what enables high end restaurants to produce dishes that home cooks really can't duplicate. They require many different preparations and either a small army of cooks working in a huge kitchen, or someone who is willing to devote several days of their life to the preparation of a single plate of food—and who is capable of doing so without any serious mistakes along the way, I should add.

## The Tools for Discovering New Flavors

When deciding to make a video, as well as in the writing of these books, my goal is always to show something that most people don't know about. Sometimes that's a technique, but I'm also a huge fan of discovering entirely new and delicious flavors because that's what my own childhood memories of food were— trips to exotic restaurants with cuisines from around the world.

If you have read my cocktail book, you already know how I took a different approach from everyone else. Rather than just a book of recipes and some nostalgic history alongside, I explained how flavors can be introduced in several different ways, the necessity of making certain ingredients yourself, and the principle of deviating from a stock recipe to create something unique and almost certainly delicious (see pages 113-115 of my cocktail book). In this series of cookbooks (I have four or five volumes in mind at this point), I'm trying to take a similar approach with food. I intend to show methods and ideas that are not in any other book, while still keeping it approachable, and (hopefully) interesting.

One of the concepts I'm introducing now in this second volume is the idea of resonant and anti-resonant ingredient pairings, which produce unexpected flavors (see page 25). This is the sort of thing you have to experience yourself to relate to. It is rather like trying to explain a new color no one has ever seen before. As one of my YouTube viewers wrote in a comment recently...

> *"Chef, I made this dish tonight. If you put a gun to my head and said to tell me what this dish tastes like or die....i would die, There are so many different flavors your tongue is confused. BUT it was very good, I will make this again." - shair00*

I will go into more detail about this in Volume 3 of this cookbook series. The next volume will also deal with the molecular chemistry of flavors even more than this one does.

## Measurement Conventions

I included this paragraph in Volume 1, but it bears repeating:

While many cooks use terms like teaspoon and tablespoon very loosely, that is not how professional chefs operate. A teaspoon (abbreviated with a lower case t) is 5 cubic centimeters, or 5ml. A tablespoon (abbreviated as an upper case T) is 15 cubic centimeters, or 15ml. Careful measurement means reproducible results, and that's vital if you are going to perfect a recipe.

## Keeping Notes and ~~Kindle~~

The single biggest difference between a home cook and a professional is simply the amount of experience. But it isn't just the sheer number of hours you spend every day, but the repetition that you get in a commercial kitchen. You are making the same set of recipes hundreds of times a week. If you discover something new, you'll try it the next time you make it—a few minutes from now! When a home cook thinks of something new to try, or realizes a mistake that they made, by the time they make the dish again—*if* they make it again—so much time has passed that they forgot the exact details of what they did last time. That's why keeping notes is extremely important—and why I did not want the publisher to release a Kindle version of these books. You need to write directly in the book so that a year or more later, you won't have the same problem. No matter how carefully and clearly I try to write, I may still have omitted an important detail. Besides, there are always issues of personal preference. Perhaps a dish was too spicy for you, or you thought it needed more of a certain ingredient. That's the advantage of paper books. Your grandchildren will still be able to read what you had to say, because Kindle may not exist in the future, but paper and ink certainly will.

Thank you for all of your support, and I hope we can continue to make this channel a success by sharing it with your friends and family in the years ahead!

# COMMERCIAL VS. HOME FREEZING

When you put food in your home freezer, the temperature drops gradually. During this time, the water in the food is turning to ice. Because it happens relatively slowly, the ice has time to form crystals which are the result of weak electromagnetic attractions between water molecules. The problem is that on a macro scale, these ice crystals are like sharp needles that puncture cell membranes—the cells that make up the vegetables and/or meat in whatever it is you are freezing.

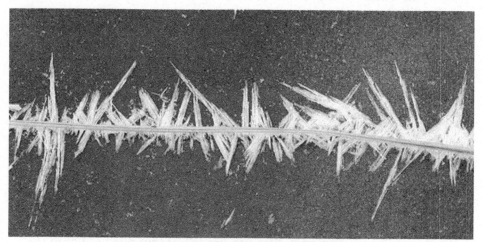

*Ice crystals when they form slowly.*

When you reheat this food later, the cells leak through the punctured holes, resulting in a mushy texture and altered flavors due to cell constituents mixing on the surface and reacting in the oxygen atmosphere they are now exposed to. Some foods are more prone to this sort of damage than others. The factors that determine what makes a food vulnerable to ice crystal damage are complicated, but suffice it to say that some damage will occur in nearly any food that you freeze yourself at home.

Commercially frozen foods are another matter, though. Industrial food processing plants freeze foods so quickly that water doesn't have time to form ice crystals. Typically food is frozen at 40° below zero, which results in water molecules simply being trapped in whatever position they happened to be in. This is called amorphous ice, and it does not exist naturally anywhere on earth. It is entirely a manmade

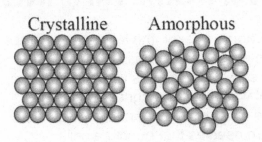

Crystalline    Amorphous

phenomenon. This causes very little damage to cell membranes, and when food is thawed out and reheated, the water becomes liquid again without ever having gone through its crystalline phase. While you can't accomplish this at home, you can help the foods you freeze have less extreme ice crystals by first refrigerating the food before you move it to the freezer. No ice will form in the refrigerator, but you have reduced the time it will take for the food to freeze by starting it off closer to the freezing point. The worst ice crystal formation and cell damage occurs when warm foods are put directly into the freezer, because ice crystals have the most time to grow in the center of foods that take the longest to chill.

Sometimes you <u>want</u> that cell damage, though! It's important for French fries and in the recipe here for the *Deep Fried Parsnips*.

## Freezing Fish for Sushi

In many countries it is a legal requirement that all fish intended for making sushi be frozen at a low temperature for enough time to kill any parasites. Typically this means 20 below zero Celsius for a minimum of 24 hours. Again, the fish is frozen commercially with the temperature dropped so rapidly that ice crystals don't have time to form. The most expensive places employ liquid nitrogen, which is about 200 degrees below zero Celsius.

On a related note, it is a common practice in the sushi industry to expose tuna to carbon monoxide gas to make it appear fresher than it is. Even though carbon monoxide is deadly to breathe, there is no danger in consuming fish that has been treated with it. First, you are eating it, not breathing it. Second, virtually all of the gas has dissipated before it gets to your plate. Without this treatment your magura sashimi would be muddy brown instead of pink.

# BRAISING

I want to begin by clarifying what braising is. It is food in a close-fitting and heavy pot that contains very little liquid. The point is that you want the liquid that comes out of the meat to be the heat conductor. You can not do that if the pot is much larger than the food it contains, or if you have put a lot of liquid in the pot. There are some misinformed "expert" TV chefs who have stated that the broth or water should come up 2/3 of the way of the vessel. That's not braising. That's simply using the oven to boil something.

Braising is an ancient method of cooking, where a vessel containing meat and vegetables was buried in a fire just as it was going out. The residual heat of the fire would slowly cook the food over a period of several hours. The advantage of this method is that the temperature starts off high and slowly decreases with time. You will find many of my recipes include a "braising schedule" where I start the oven off at a higher temperature, and tell you to turn it down after some period of time, and sometimes even a third temperature after another couple of hours. This is a true braise, and generally produces the best results.

The utilitarian advantage of a braise is that it enables one to transform very tough cuts of meat into something palatable. This would have been especially important long ago, because the meat from the working muscles of wild game animals is like leather if you try to cook it quickly.

The *doufeu* pot is a curious invention made by Le Creuset that bears mentioning. The idea is that you put ice in the recessed lid on top in order to promote condensation. This half-baked idea (pun intended) is ridiculous because the ice quickly turns into steaming water in the oven. Very quickly.

## Size Matters (and Smaller is Better)

A braise needs to be carried out in a close-fitting vessel to maximize the concentration of the vapors. Imagine a braising pot the size of a football stadium. It might as well be open air. That's an exaggeration of the same problem you face by using a pot that is much larger than the food being braised.

## Can I Use a Crock Pot Instead?

*No!* There are several reasons, any one of which would be sufficient grounds to dismiss crock pots as being a viable alternative. First, modern crock pots operate at a temperature that is too high for most braising applications. Second, the surface is being heated electrically. If there is no liquid behind the surface, it gets very hot inside. If you do fill it with liquid, you are stewing—not braising. Third, most people have a single size of crock pot, but a proper braise needs to be done in a close-fitting vessel. I have yet to meet a professional chef who likes crock pots for anything other than keeping soup hot. When it comes to braising, there is no substitute for the well regulated low temperature inside of an oven.

## Can I Use a Pressure Cooker Instead?

*No!* I explained this on page 22 of Volume 1.

## Equivalent of a Braise in Organic Chemistry

A standard method for carrying out a chemical synthesis in an organic laboratory is called a *reflux*. This consists of heating a solution of reactants in a solvent to the boiling point in a flask fitted with a water-cooled condenser so that all of the vapors run back down into the boiling solution, rather than being able to escape into the atmosphere. Equipped with a good condenser, a reaction can proceed for days, or even longer without any loss of the original volume of material. The purpose of this is to allow chemical reactions to take place in a controlled manner.

Many reactions simply take time because they involve a specific collision of molecules that are statistically unlikely. Only a small percentage will take place per hour. If you heat it up more you get unwanted side reactions instead of the intended products. There is some percentage of undesirable reactions in an organic reaction no matter what you do, but you minimize those by the careful and even application of heat. This is exactly what you are doing in a braise.

# FLAVOR CHEMISTRY

For over a century it was believed that the tongue is only capable of detecting four flavors (sweet, salty, bitter and sour)—or five if you count savory (umami)—and each type of sensor is located in a different region on the tongue. We now know that the old "geography map" of the tongue is pseudoscience. The limited number of tastes we can detect with our tongues may be scientifically correct, but we taste food with more than just our tongues. In fact, most of the taste of our food actually comes from the olfactory system in our nose. This is why you can hardly taste anything if you have a bad head cold. Your tongue isn't affected.

So let's put this archaic and counterproductive argument to rest. It is an indisputable fact that human beings can taste a vast array of flavors. Some people more than others, but that's another topic. Furthermore, our tastes become more refined with more exposure to foods. An example of this is how Asian people can discriminate between brands of white rice that seem absolutely identical to western palates, or how many Italians can tell you whether a pasta was cut using a bronze die or a steel die. The brain has an astounding ability to recognize tiny variations once it's conditioned to do so.

The variations that our senses are responding to is an orchestra of molecular flavor components. We can think of each type of molecule as a musical instrument playing its own part of the overall harmony. Listened to by itself, the composition may be totally unrecognizable, but as part of the symphony, each instrument plays an important part. Only even a large philharmonic orchestra is extremely simplistic compared to the vast array of components present in most foods. After all, in an orchestra there are entire sections of strings and brass that simply play in unison. In foods, very few molecules are identical in taste and aroma—and it is not unusual for more than a hundred such molecules to be collectively responsible for the overall taste that we experience. Perhaps more difficult to appreciate is how so often none of the individual molecular components taste anything like the food as a whole.

In fact, there are very few exceptions to this rule. Vanilla is one such exception, where 4-Hydroxy-3-methoxybenzaldehyde (better known as Vanillin) actually smells like vanilla all by itself. Because of this, food manufacturers prefer to use the far less expensive Vanillin rather than the natural product. By the way, just because you see brown flecks in your vanilla ice cream, it doesn't mean the maker used the corresponding amount of real vanilla beans. The husks of the vanilla bean plant (which are nearly flavorless) are sold cheap to food manufacturers for use in such deception. It is perfectly legal. Real vanilla contains hundreds of different chemical components. Artificial "vanilla extract" contains only the one component, Vanillin, dissolved in alcohol. But that's old school food chemistry. These days things are much more sophisticated. More than the average consumer could even imagine.

## Bacon Chemistry

The chemical analysis of molecular flavor components has created a whole world of artificial flavors that are known only by their chemical names, and generally used only by food

Six important chemicals found in the aroma of bacon being cooked that are also used as artificial flavorings.

| Molecular Component | Aroma / Taste | Commercial Uses / Notes |
|---|---|---|
| 2,3-dimethylpyrazine | Cocoa, roasted nuts, slightly fatty | Condiments, soups, convenience foods |
| 2,5-dimethylpyrazine | Roasted meat, coffee | Seasonings, soups, meats, fast food |
| 2-ethyl-5-methylpyrazine | Roasted nuts, grass | Flavoring agent, found in dark beers |
| 2-ethyl-3,5-dimethylpyrazine | Hazel nuts, overtones of cocoa and fat | Desserts, candies, flavorings |
| 2-pentylfuran | Green beans, vegetable, savory flavor | Herb/spice blends, dips, found in coffee |
| 3,4-dimethylpyridine | Nutty aroma in low concentrations | Flavorings, found in coal tar and shale |

2,3-dimethylpyrazine

2,5-dimethylpyrazine

2-ethyl-5-methylpyrazine

2-pentylfuran

3,4-dimethylpyridine (also known as lutidine)

manufacturers (with the exception of a few trendy chefs who specialize in molecular gastronomy and directly add laboratory chemicals to their dishes).

One of the most alluring aromas to analyze early on was the smell of bacon as it cooks. Although there is a vast panoply of molecules responsible for all of the subtle nuances, six molecules were identified as the most important key components (see the table on the opposite page). Each of these molecules is now used by food manufacturers in a vast array of products. Some examples are listed on that table. Note that none of those components smells or tastes distinctly like bacon by itself. There is no single molecule that resembles the olfactory symphony of bacon being cooked.

There is no physical difference between the chemical flavor molecules that are manufactured through industrial chemical synthesis and the same molecule that's naturally present in foods. They are absolutely identical. The folklore that "natural chemicals" are different from synthetic chemicals is pure ignorance. The problem is that the ratio of these components is now being manipulated artificially, and there are health risks including cancer with some of these materials. So a natural food product may contain carcinogenic compounds, but only a tiny fraction of the amount that is added by a commercial manufacturer as an artificial flavoring.

At this point you might be thinking that it is hypocritical of me to fault food manufacturers for their use of such chemicals while I endorse the use of MSG. Glutamate is a natural compound in the human body. Ingesting a little as a seasoning in food has been found to be completely safe in every clinical trial that has ever been done—and there have been many such studies. It is not carcinogenic, either. See pages 17-18 of Volume 1 and pages 222-223 of this book for more about the proof that MSG is safe.

You may also be wondering why food manufacturers would add such chemicals to their products in the first place. There are two main reasons. The main reason is that this enables them to use poor quality meats and produce—sometimes even spoiled—and then bring it back to life as a kind of Franken-food by bleaching, coloring and artificially flavoring it. For many years I lived near two large food manufacturing plants. Both are well known American brands. One made potato chips and the other canned tomato sauce. We could see truckloads of rotten, spoiled tomatoes being delivered all the time. When freight cars of potatoes would arrive to the factory, they were slimy and gray. The smell was so bad that it made you want to vomit even from a quarter mile away. How does that get turned into something delicious? With a whole lot of processing. That's not how things are done everywhere, though.

*San Marzano tomatoes growing in Italy.*

## Tomato Chemistry

In the first volume of this cookbook series, I devoted a couple of pages to extolling the virtues of Italian pasata and San Marzano tomatoes. As is so often the case in life, you tend to get what you pay for. If you are buying the cheapest tomato sauce you can, the chances are it will have been made with horribly bad tomatoes and then reincarnated through chemical manipulation. Often the only visible warning on the can is the price sticker. Bon appétit.

We have only just scratched the surface of the complexity of this topic. The next thing to consider is the natural variation in specific chemical components present in our molecular orchestra. That is, how loud each instrument is playing. Even within one specific subspecies of plant, there can be a remarkable range (thousands of fold) in specific flavor components. Consider the chart below.

Observed Variation in Flavor Volatiles within *S. lycopersicum* Heirloom Varietie

| Molecular Component | High | Low | Fold Difference | Median | Aroma / Taste |
|---|---|---|---|---|---|
| 1-penten-3-one | 9.37 | 0.17 | 55 | 1.18 | Pungent pepper, mustard, garlic |
| isovaleronitrile | 68.45 | 0.58 | 117 | 7.63 | (no available data) |
| *trans*-2-pentenal | 5.16 | 0.31 | 17 | 1.23 | Reminiscent of green apple |
| *trans*-2-heptenal | 2.71 | 0.09 | 30 | 0.42 | Oily fat with a hint of sweet fruit |
| isovaleraldehyde | 51.08 | 1.55 | 33 | 8.59 | High notes of chocolate and peach |
| 3-methyl-1-butanol | 184.46 | 3.20 | 58 | 27.26 | Alcohol; reminiscent of whiskey |
| methional | 1.616 | 0.012 | 137 | 0.07 | Potato skins, musty and slightly meaty |
| isovaleric acid | 0.953 | 0.004 | 262 | 0.09 | Sweaty feet, locker room |
| 2-isobutylthiazole | 63.61 | 0.37 | 174 | 8.34 | * Tomato leaves, waxy, metallic |
| 6-methyl-5-hepten-2-one | 20.07 | 0.17 | 120 | 3.38 | Hints of green beans and banana |
| β-ionone | 0.396 | 0.008 | 47 | 0.05 | Woody, tropical, berries, beeswax |
| phenylacetaldehyde | 1.90 | 0.00 | 654 | 0.24 | Honey, roses, baby powder |
| geranylacetone | 28.96 | 0.03 | 1,095 | 1.22 | Rose leaves and magnolia tree |
| 2-phenylethanol | 5.269 | 0.002 | 3,142 | 0.05 | Dried roses with a hint of bread |
| isobutyl acetate | 11.93 | 0.14 | 85 | 1.67 | Banana and tutti frutti |
| *cis*-3-hexen-1-ol | 124.15 | 10.00 | 12 | 40.00 | Fresh cut grass |
| 1-nitro-2-phenylethane | 2.59 | 0.02 | 149 | 0.25 | Warm spice |
| *trans,trans*-2,4-decadienal | 0.30 | 0.00 | 211 | 0.02 | Chicken fat with a hint of coriander |
| 2-methylbutanal | 14.66 | 1.14 | 13 | 3.47 | Nuts, corn cobs |
| hexyl alcohol | 84.03 | 0.99 | 85 | 13.86 | Pungent, alcohol, fuel oil |
| guaiacol | 8.09 | 0.03 | 290 | 0.77 | Smoke, wood, vanilla |
| hexanal | 381.05 | 15.55 | 25 | 88.65 | Grassy, citrus, lingering aftertaste |
| 1-octen-3-one | 0.312 | 0.017 | 18 | 0.07 | Mushrooms, cabbage |
| *cis*-3-hexenal | 399.66 | 8.29 | 48 | 71.09 | Fresh cut grass and green apples |
| methylsalicylate | 14.16 | 0.00 | 3,354 | 0.40 | Wintergreen, mint |
| *trans*-2-hexenal | 48.01 | 0.39 | 123 | 3.54 | Unripe green banana but also fatty |
| β-damascenone | 0.1733 | 0.0020 | 86 | 0.01 | Sweet plum, grape, raspberry |
| 2-methyl-1-butanol | 115.69 | 1.93 | 60 | 15.08 | Alcohol, faintly like smoked salmon |

Volatile emissions were measured as ng/g fresh weight/hr.

First notice that of the 28 components considered to be the most important contributors of tomato aroma and taste, only one of them is individually tomato-like, and that's mostly the aroma in the leaves that we don't eat. Despite the considerable variation in the concentration of different specific components, you can be sure that any one of the tomatoes that were part of this analysis would have smelled and tasted like a "tomato". The difference is that some of those tomatoes would have smelled and tasted much better than others. You may have never heard of any of these chemicals before, but your olfactory sensors and brain are wired to respond to them, and they use this information to decide what will be nutritious and delicious. So, a food manufacturer that manipulates the balance of these components can fool your senses into thinking that something is scrumptious when in fact it is reconstituted spoiled vegetation that would have only been good for compost before this technology existed.

However, this knowledge has other applications than just tricking consumers into buying low quality foodstuffs. It has also unlocked some valuable keys to producing better quality wines by knowing how to blend different varieties with greater precision than was ever possible before. For more about this, see "The Grapes of Math" (page 86) of my book, *40 Years in One Night*, if you have it.

Furthermore, this understanding provides a whole new way of thinking about how foods taste. The organic molecules that are responsible for the taste of one particular food, are often present in other unrelated foods. The balance of those components is altered by the time and temperature of cooking, as well as what else was present during the cooking. An example of the latter is the abundance of turmeric in the original British curry powder mixes (see pages 41-42). One of the most interesting ways to exploit this in a natural way (without directly adding chemicals) is by the use of dried vegetables and fruits as seasonings. While this is impossible to apply by direct design without some very expensive equipment, it is useful to keep in mind what it is you are doing when you add together components that were cooked in different ways. You are reinforcing some flavor molecules, and lowering the overall concentration of others. Just keeping it in mind when you are experimenting with combining flavors will open a new dimension of tastes. This is the most intriguing thing about food chemistry—it has the potential to create new never-before-tasted flavors that are incredibly delicious. This is what I strive for in my recipes.

For more technical reading on this topic, see the unfortunately titled book, "Odors in the Food Industry", by Xaviar Nicolay. Published by Springer (2006).

# DRIED VS. FREEZE DRIED HERBS

Most of the dried herbs that you purchase in packages and bottles are freeze dried, which is very different from drying herbs yourself. As I just showed in the previous chapter, the aroma and flavor of natural products is comprised of dozens of individual chemical compounds. Some of these components are more volatile than others. Certain herbs have key flavor molecules that can't be preserved very well even by freeze drying. Basil is a prime example of this. There is no such thing as dry basil that smells or tastes very much like fresh basil. Still, dried basil is useful from time to time. Just don't think of it as a substitute for fresh basil. The same is true for freeze dried cilantro and mint. They are pale shadows of the fresh form.

Chives and dill are at the opposite end of the spectrum, being seemingly more intense in their freeze dried form than when fresh picked, though the flavor profiles are not the same.

Dried tarragon and chervil are all over the map—ranging from very weak to very strong, depending on the manufacturer.

When you dry herbs in an oven, you drive off even more of the volatile components than in the freeze drying process. Sometimes that can be a good thing. The most useful herb for this approach is sage. Normally sage is very potent. It can easily overpower foods, especially when it is in the raw leaf form. Sage is one of my favorite herbs to deep fry and use as a garnish, but deep fried sage is often *too* subdued. Sometimes you want some of the notes of sage, but you don't want to cook sprigs of it into the dish, because then it would flavor everything. You want small flecks of sage to show up in bites serendipitously. That's when you can crumble over oven-dried sage. An example of this is the recipe here for *Campanelle with Braised Cabbage, Mustard and Sage* (page 64).

Other herbs that lend themselves to being oven dried to bring their potency under control include lovage, marjoram and shiso.

# GROUND DRIED VEGETABLES AND FRUITS AS SEASONINGS

Aside from the ubiquitous dried chili pepper, many other fruits and vegetables can be turned into intriguing seasonings through dry roasting them. Dried celery and celery salt (a mixture of dried celery with salt) is available in many large grocery stores. What is surprising is that some other dried vegetables that are common in Russia are almost nonexistent as a commercially made product elsewhere. For instance dried carrots and dried celery root are sold in inexpensive packets, as shown in the photo below.

However, these products are freeze dried, not roasted. As such, they do not have the same type of flavor that is achieved by the overnight roasting process that I am advocating. Also, Russians are certainly not grinding these up and using them as seasonings, I assure you! They use them in soups, particularly for camping trips and during the summer months where many spend outside of the cities and fresh vegetables are not available in the tiny convenience stores in dacha villages.

I first became aware of the possibilities of dried vegetables as seasonings as a child back when companies provided a more complete list of actual ingredients, rather than vague terms like "natural and artificial flavorings". For more about this, see the text under "Dried Beets" in the recipe *1890's Meat Sauce* (page 108).

## General Scheme

Place the material to be dried in the oven set to 80°C (175°F) with the fan assist ON and let it run 8-14 hours, depending on the size of the pieces and how moist they are. When testing to see if it is really dry, remove the tray and let the pieces rest at room temperature uncovered for about 10 minutes. Then if there is a clean snap when you try to break a piece in two, they are done. If they bend like leather, then they still need more drying time.

## Paprika

Just as you can dry your own chili peppers, as I covered in Volume 1 of this series, you can also produce your own paprika if you have the right peppers. That's what I do in the *Transylvanian Tochitură* recipe (page 148). However, there is one more twist to this that is not explained in that video. If you dry the peppers at a constant temperature of 70-80°C (about 170°F) with fan assist on until they are completely dry, you will get what is known as "sweet paprika". If, after about 80% of the drying time you increase the heat to 120°C (250°C) for 1-2 hours, you will get "bittersweet paprika", which has an aroma reminiscent of coffee. Although the sweet paprika is generally more useful, there are times where bittersweet paprika is better suited. For example, I almost always select the bittersweet variety for goat dishes. Both types lose flavor fairly soon after grinding, so keep the dried peppers whole in a closed container in your refrigerator for maximum shelf life.

## Tomatoes

Tomatoes are rich in umami, but you don't always want something tasting like tomato just to get a savory taste in the dish. Here's where the magical transformation of dry roasting comes to play. Tomatoes that have been dried and powdered have their own unique flavor (more similar to a dried pepper) but still pack a load of umami flavor due in part to their natural glutamate content.

*23*

The taste sensation we describe as savory (the Japanese word is umami) arises when certain receptors on the tongue are stimulated. Glutamate (MSG) is a primary source of this reaction. Flip to the back of this book on pages 222-223 to see the amount of MSG naturally present in tomatoes and some other foods.

## To Salt or Not to Salt?

Salting the vegetables before you put them in the oven them will speed the drying process some, but it also means you will have a salty product that can make controlling the amount of salt in the final dish difficult. Also, in some instances adding salt to vegetables has a distinct effect on how they taste after drying. To be safe, don't add salt unless specifically instructed to.

## Plums

While most fruits don't do well on dry roasting—and some are horrible beyond belief, such as watermelon and strawberries—a few fruits do lend themselves to this treatment. Most especially plums. Although prunes are dried plums, dry roasted plums are completely different because prunes are not roasted at a high temperature, or to the point of being so brittle that they can be powdered. You can sometimes purchase dried plums (not prunes), to save time, but they are still a bit leathery and not sufficiently roasted to be grindable. The final product tastes more like an exotic brown sugar than it does either plums or prunes. Here again salting will produce a different product, and is only applicable if you are starting with the fresh fruit. Only add salt if the recipe says, "dried salted plums", which is mostly useful for fish dishes.

Note that Japanese *umeboshi*, often translated as "dried plums", or "dried salted plums" are entirely different, being pickled. They are not suitable for this method of dry roasting.

# FLAVOR RESONANCE

There are certain flavor pairings that amplify nature itself. These are so natural that it is nearly impossible to achieve a great flavor without using them as a pair. Some things like salt, pepper, MSG and aromatic vegetables (onions, garlic, celery, carrots and peppers) are universal matches with virtually all savory dishes. Below are some examples of other well established symbiotic pairings, many of which you are undoubtedly familiar with:

| | |
|---|---|
| Chicken | Thyme, Lemon |
| Turkey | Sage, Smoke |
| Duck | Orange, Almond |
| Lamb | Mint, Pomegranate |
| Beef | Red Wine, Mushrooms |
| Ham | Cloves, Pineapple |
| Salmon | Dill, Caviar |
| White Fish | Fennel, Anise (or Pernod) |
| Seafood | Lemon, Butter |
| Tomatoes | Basil, Olive Oil |
| Artichokes | Hard Cheeses, Lemon |
| Apples | Cinnamon, Brown Sugar |

The reason for these is understandable through the chemistry of their molecular flavor components, but it is very complicated to explain. As an example, if you try to make a chicken dish (see chart above) with citric acid for lemon juice and substituting thyme with thymol (the chief chemical components of lemon and thyme, respectively), the result is very mediocre, because the "magic" lies in all the dozens of other chemical components that are found in the natural products of lemon juice and thyme.

However, chemical analysis can turn up some interesting combinations that might not have occurred to us otherwise. So can using your own sense of taste and thinking about what other flavors you can taste in something in the same language that a wine enthusiast uses. You have an incredibly powerful piece of analytical equipment right in your own head and with a little practice, by actually thinking about what you are tasting you may discover pairings that amplify each other—which is what a symbiotic pairing does. It could be almost anything.

### Advanced Topic: Parallel and Anti-Resonance

There are also pairings that cancel the expected overall flavor and create something new and unfamiliar. Parallel resonance is between genetically related plants (*e.g.* cabbage and mustard) or things processed differently and combined. Anti-resonance is so dissimilar that a cloud of flavor molecules create interference. These work like the Complexing Agents in my book, *Cocktails of the South Pacific and Beyond.* Tasted individually, these mixtures are often strange and even downright unpleasant—just as you wouldn't drink Angostura bitters straight out of the bottle, but combined with other ingredients, the effect can be stunning. Sometimes a problem is a different expectation of taste, so someone will perceive it negatively because it isn't what they thought it would be like. Such combinations are best concealed so that the diner tastes what is novel without any preconceptions clouding their judgement, as in these examples.

| | | |
|---|---|---|
| Cabbage | Mustard Seeds | *Campanelle with Cabbage*<br>Page 64 |
| Cherries | Sichuan Pepper | *Starlight Meatballs*<br>Page 128 |
| Blue Cheese | Absinthe | *Bavarian Blue Frog Legs*<br>Page 120 |
| Eggplant | Marjoram | *Italian Eggplant Sandwich*<br>Page 176 |

*A tiny bit*

# ~~ALL~~ ABOUT WINES

The topic of wines is extremely involved. Wine making is an ancient art and the appreciation of fine wine is a learned skill that most people never acquire. However, you don't need to be a licensed sommelier to know what you like, or to know which wine to select for cooking. Here is some *practical* advice for the novice...

## The Percentage of Alcohol Rule of Thumb

I know most serious wine enthusiasts would cringe at the following generalization, but I don't care because the fact remains that it is true almost without exception: A high alcohol concentration is almost always an indication of a wine's strong characteristic taste. That is, an 11% alcohol wine will taste very thin and weak when compared to a wine with just 1% more alcohol.

A wine with an alcohol level of 14.5% will almost always be rich and vibrant. Yes, there are some exceptions where a 13% wine can blow you away, and a 14.5% wine is disappointing, but if you are in a wine shop and clueless, this rule of thumb will <u>rarely</u> disappoint. If you want something that you can drink like water, then go for the low alcohol. If you want a wine that is going to stand up to a steak smothered in roasted red chili peppers, then find the label boasting the highest percentage of alcohol in the shop.

## Fortified Wines

So you think you have found the most amazingly potent wine ever produced. The label states it has 19% alcohol by volume. What you are almost certainly looking at is a *fortified wine*. The most common of these include sherry, port, marsala, madeira and vermouth. These are wines in which a strong liquor (usually brandy) has been added either during or after the fermentation. These are distinct styles of wine that are very common in cooking, but are completely different from red and white table wines.

Although vermouth is commonly produced in both dry (white) and sweet (red) varieties, the red is almost never used in cooking.

Dry white vermouth is essentially a modest quality white wine with an infusion of herbs. If you seldom drink white wine, dry vermouth is a good product to keep on hand for cooking because it has an extremely long shelf life (even after opening) and the herbal notes are rarely objectionable, providing that only a small amount is used. Vermouth won't always work, though. Don't use vermouth to make Sauce Béarnaise, for instance.

Fortified wines have many subtypes, too. Sherry ranges in tastes from very dry (fino) to medium-heavy (oloroso), all the way to rich and sweet (amoltino). Port can be either white or red, and also has distinct subtypes such as ruby and tawny. Trying to explain the difference in flavor between these in words is quite impossible. If you aren't familiar with them and you are serious about cooking, accumulate bottles of each type—taste and learn. Fortified wines have extremely long shelf lives, so you can maintain a library of them without going broke.

There is a substitute for port, but it is still wine. There are some semi-sweet red wines that can imitate port in cooking if you add about 10% volume of sugar to them (50 grams sugar per 500ml of wine), although the optimum amount will depend on the specific wine. See my *Port Wine BBQ Sauce* recipe (page 134).

Along with dry red and white wine, these are all crucial ingredients in European cuisine, from the lowliest peasant stew to the signature dishes in Michelin 3-star restaurants. Not understanding these basic flavors is like trying to compose music without knowing what the instruments sound like. There is no substitute for wine in any dish. Period.

## Abstaining from Alcohol in Foods? Do the Math

I have explained this before in the comments section of videos, but it bears repeating: There is more alcohol in a piece of ripe fruit than there is in almost any portion of food that was cooked with wine or spirits, because nearly all of the alcohol evaporates during the cooking process. For example, a ripe banana or a glass of orange juice each contain the same amount of pure alcohol as in about 20ml (3/4 ounce) of wine. That's wine *before* you cook it, mind you! Cooking removes over 90% of the alcohol (and more than that if you also flambé it), which means that your glass of orange juice has <u>more</u> alcohol in it than an entire bottle of wine in a recipe that makes four portions. If you think you are avoiding alcohol by not eating foods cooked with wine, you are only fooling yourself. This is also why it is perfectly legal to serve children foods cooked with wine in restaurants. Same thing for other spirits.

## Selecting Wines for Cooking

What quality of wine should be used in a recipe is a question that I get asked frequently. There are three traditional responses to this. The first is to use the cheapest wine you can find, because "you can't tell the difference in the final cooked dish". This is only true if the people tasting the dish can't tell the difference between cheap wine and good wine. The flavor will absolutely carry through, and unfortunately the bad notes that define a cheap wine will be amplified as it reduces.

At the opposite end of this stance is the advice that you should always use the finest wine that you can possibly afford. That's excellent advice if you are the personal chef to the king and want to be sure you aren't beheaded for insubordination. Otherwise this is simply excess to the point of being ridiculous.

The third adage is to only use a wine that you would actually drink yourself. This is a good rule of thumb if you drink good wine. If you are not a wine drinker and just buy whatever is on sale at a convenience store for a holiday, then it might be time to expand your awareness about wines. See **Wines for Drinking** (below).

For white wine in cooking, you can't ask for a better value or finer choice than Oyster Bay Chardonnay from New Zealand. My second choice for a white wine is Santa Rita Reserva Chardonnay from Casablanca Valley, Chile.

When it comes to dry red wine in cooking, in most instances the best choice will be a Cabernet from Chili with an alcohol level of 14% or more. If you need something more refined, move up to a good Pinot Noir from California, also watching to be sure the alcohol is 14% minimum. The exceptions to this simplistic rule are when you are preparing classic French or Italian dishes, in which case there may well be an advantage to using something from the region the dish originated in. From a practical standpoint, very few people will have any idea that you substituted a Chilean Cabernet for a French Bordeaux if you don't tell them. Restaurants frequently cheat by using only a small portion of the expensive wine mentioned on the menu and 90% or more of a less expensive wine. Legally they have included the ingredient specified, but of course that's not what the customer imagines that they're getting. Very few customers would be able to tell even if you gave them side-by-side versions to compare. This scam does not apply to the finest restaurants, though. Once again, you get what you pay for.

## Wines for Drinking

If you are already familiar with wines to some extent, then forgive me for what I'm about to do. Namely, to distill down an encyclopedia of information about wines into a couple of paragraphs of practical advice for the novice.

I give you my list of the five most accessible and distinctive varietals to become familiar with...

---

**CHARDONNAY**

Rich and buttery when aged in oak. Otherwise more citrus and crisp mineral taste. Barrel aging is declared on the label.

**RIESLING**

Sweeter and lighter white than Chardonnay. German rieslings are especially sweet. Alsatian rieslings have more depth.

**CABERNET SAUVIGNON**

The king of red wines, but because of the demand and difficulty in production, Cabernet tends to be really overpriced. Cabernet from Chile is a far better value than from California.

**PINOT NOIR**

This can be as full bodied as a Cabernet, but a better value. Pinot Noir varies tremendously, from thin and watery to deep and almost ink-liike. Again, you get what you pay for.

**ZINFANDEL**

A deep, rich and fruit-forward red varietal that can be a massive powerhouse of flavor. Known as Primativo in Italy.

---

This list is like a snowflake resting on top of the tip of the iceberg, but you have to start somewhere. You can't be a serious cook without having at least a rudimentary knowledge of wine.

## New World vs. Old World Wines

These are two completely different schools of thought. European wines are usually labeled by their terroir—the geographic region that they came from. A single bottle may contain half a dozen different types of grapes, but they were all grown in that particular region. Contrast this with New World (Napa, Chile, Australia, South Africa), where a wine is generally made with only one type of grape, but may be from several different regions. New World wines are generally stronger in flavor and a better value.

## Tasting Wines as an Olfactory Exercise

Most of the "flavor" of wine is actually in the nose—the aroma. You can prove this to yourself by pinching your nose and tasting any wine you like. Our sense of smell is far more sophisticated than our sense of taste. The first step in learning to appreciate wine is in being consciously aware of the isolated aroma. You play a sort of question and answer game with yourself as you sniff the bouquet of the wine. Can you smell citrus? If so, is it lemon? Orange? Orange blossoms? Can you smell watermelon? Raspberry? Vanilla? Mint? You think about these aromas in your mind and then see if you can find a match. You'll be surprised at how many different scents can be detected in a good wine, and also how lacking in complexity a cheap wine is. That's why good wines sell for more. Not that all wines are priced fairly, of course. Many are overpriced, and some are undervalued. However, the *general trend* is... (yes, I'm saying it again) ...you get what you pay for. You aren't going to find an expensive wine that tastes awful, nor are you going to find a cheap wine that surpasses the flavor of a very expensive one.

One of the best things about becoming familiar with tasting wines is that those same skills apply to cooking. With practice, you can judge your own food better and mentally contemplate what can be done to improve it just by tasting in your own mind. What would this have tasted like with more thyme? What if I had used green peppercorns instead of black? ...and so on.

## Sommelier or Con Artist?

Sommeliers are easy targets for ridicule. First, because it's impossible to present yourself as a superior authority on wines (or anything else) without looking at least a little pompous. To make matters worse, the nature of the job requires that they dress well beyond their tax bracket. You know that when closing time comes, this penguin-esque character changes back into his Levis and drives his banged up compact car home to a small apartment. All too often they come across like a grifter trying to unload high-profit wines on an unsuspecting mark—and even if you know a lot about wine, you are socially obligated to play along. The reason is that the appointed sommelier is not always a certified expert. Some are exactly what they appear to be: A sort of used car salesman for the restaurant who derives part of his pay by moving the wines with the widest profit margin. Just don't think that's *always* the case. Try looking into becoming a certified sommelier and you'll quickly realize that this is a serious course of study that takes many years.

For these reasons they tend to have a bad reputation, but there is a big problem with the field itself even for gifted, knowledgeable and licensed sommeliers. Namely, the average person does not appreciate the complexity and characteristics of wines that are prized by experts. There is a huge gap between what the general public loves and what someone who has spent years developing an appreciation for wines will drink. Often they are exact opposites. Many people enjoy wines that are quite sweet, not strong, and lack any real character. So when a sommelier suggests a wine that isn't sweet, has a higher alcohol concentration than the guest is accustomed to, and has a pronounced character that was selected to compliment their food, the guest is often left feeling ripped off for having been steered toward this "overpriced nasty sour wine", or (perhaps worse) they feel dumb for being unable to appreciate why this wine is better than the cheap stuff they usually guzzle. Appreciating wine is an actual skill.

## The Illusion of Price

The bottom line is that wine appreciation does not happen simply by ordering an expensive bottle once in a blue moon. It is a hobby for the affluent, but also something of a requirement for a top chef—and be warned, once you develop a taste for expensive wines, you will never be happy with inexpensive wines again.

There are some videos on YouTube and stories that claim wine experts usually fail blind tastings, and that when they are told that a wine they are tasting is very expensive, they will give it a good rating even if it is actually rotgut. These stories are either completely false, or they are misleading because they omit details about how these surveys were conducted. Wine tasting events are often open to the public. Just because someone is at one of these events doesn't qualify them as an expert. So getting opinions from a random sampling of participants is not the same thing as a selection of knowledgeable experts.

A particular person failing to accurately assess an unknown sample does not mean that wine tasting is subjective and arbitrary. It is a scientific fact that different wines contain different balances of molecular flavor components. Gas chromatography (a type of chemical analysis) of any wine will produce cold hard **proof**. There is nothing subjective about those figures. Although there are learned skills involved, some people are just naturally better at sensing those variations than others. If you think Coke and Pepsi taste the same, you will never be a sommelier.

I have participated in countless wine tastings, and the idea of confusing cheap wine with a good wine is about as likely as confusing water with apple juice. It isn't being a "wine snob" any more than someone spitting out sour milk is a "dairy snob".

## Wine Glasses

There are no less than a dozen different styles of glassware marketed for specific types of wines. Stemless glasses have also became stylish, but your hand warms the wine that way with detrimental effects. Stemware was invented for a good reason. In general, big flavors go in big glasses. Champagne in flutes to slow the release of the bubbles. That's all you really need to know. This advice comes to you from Christian Broder, a respected certified level-two sommelier whose father was a food chemist.

# INDIAN INGREDIENTS

While many ingredients used in Indian cooking are also well known in western cooking such as chilies, onions, garlic, ginger, coriander and cumin, other items are often poorly understood. Here are some of the more common ingredients you are likely to find...

| ENGLISH NAME | INDIAN NAMES | FAMILY / NOTES |
|---|---|---|
| Ajwain or Carom Seeds | Ajvan | Parsley family / Northern India Spice version of the herb thyme. |
| Amchoor or Dried Mango Powder | Amchur | Cashew family / Souring agent used like citric acid and sumac. |
| Asafoetida | Hing | Parsley family / South India Pungent sulfur aroma and taste. |
| Cardamom Pods | Chhoti Elaichi (green) Kali Elaichi | Ginger family / Green and black are completely different in taste |
| Caraway Seeds | Shahi jeera or Zeru (Punjabi) | Parsley family / Northern India Confused with black cumin |
| Cinnamon | Dalchini | Laurel family / Usually confused with cassia (see more below) |
| Curry Leaves | Karipatta | Citrus family / Dried have very little flavor compared to fresh |
| Dagarful or Black Stone Flower | Dagad Phool or Kalpasi | Lichen / South India, especially Chettinad cuisine |
| Fenugreek Leaves and Seeds | Methi | Fabaceae (bean family) / Common throughout India |
| Kapok Buds | Marathi Moggu or Shalmali | Mallows family / South India, especially Chettinad cuisine |
| Mace | Javitri | Nutmeg family / From the outer coating of the nutmeg fruit. |
| Mustard Oil and Seeds | Sarson (yellow) and Rai (brown) | Cabbage family / Mustard oil is especially used in Bengal |
| Nigella, Charnushka or Black Cumin | Kalaunji | Buttercup family / Frequently mislabeled as black onion seed |
| Pomegranate Seeds | Anardana | Pomegranate family / Fruity and sour, also used in Middle East |
| Poppy Seeds | Aphim posta or Khaskhas (Punjabi) | Poppy family / Especially in Bengali and Mughlai cuisines |
| Tamarind | Imli | Caesalpiniaceae family (tropical bean family) / Tart and fruity |
| Turmeric | Haldi | Ginger family / Widely used in India and British curry powders |

# * Additional Information *

**Ajwain, or Carom Seeds**: Most similar to thyme in both aroma and chemical composition. The component oils are quite volatile, so this should be ground fresh and added at the end of cooking, otherwise it will contribute little or no flavor to the dish.

**Amchoor**: In Indian cuisine (especially vegetarian dishes), amchoor is a common source of the sour component in balancing the flavors of a dish. Other sources of sour include lemon juice, vinegar, tamarind and citric acid. Of these, citric acid is the most pure form of acidity (see pages 44-45 for more about citric acid). Amchoor is made from unripe mango, so as you would expect, there are fruity notes along with the acidity, although not as much fruit as with tamarind.

**Asafoetida**: This is the probably the most difficult Indian spice to understand because it is in a category that has no equivalent in western cuisine. In a word, it is sulfer-like. The other Indian spice in this category is Black Cardamom, though not nearly as powerful. Asafoetida smells something like a cross between burning tires and model airplane glue. Of course it doesn't taste like that in the final dish. It mellows and changes on cooking. It has the medicinal property of relieving intestinal gas, so it is almost always added to Indian bean and legume dishes. There are religious orders in India that forbid the consumption of garlic, and so asafoetida became an integral part of those cuisines, being the next best thing to garlic (though only vaguely similar). Asafoetida is never a primary seasoning. It is only a minor player in rounding out complex spice mixtures. When it is fresh you need to store the opened bottle inside of another sealed glass jar to keep it from contaminating your entire kitchen.

**Cardamom Pods (Green)**: A little known fact about green cardamom is that the concentration of flavor is extremely variable, ranging from faint to overwhelming. This makes it impossible to reliably state how much should be put in a recipe. It varies by the age of the pods and how they have been stored, and probably other factors, too. You have to use your own judgement, and if your cardamom is potent, then use less.

**Cardamom Pods (Black)**: Also called Brown Cardamom sometimes. This has a smoky sulfury odor that is only useful for savory dishes, particularly lamb and mutton. It is completely different from green cardamom, except for one thing: Both have husks that will not dissolve into food no matter how long they cook. In the case of green cardamom, you can crack them open and use only the tiny little seeds inside. This will eliminate a lot of the flavor, but at least you won't have what seems like fragments of wood in your final dish. This is not an option with black cardamom, though. Most of the flavor is in that outside shell. So you either pass the sauce through a sieve at some point to get rid of those bits, or you just accept that it has some pithy bits in it, which is what Indians generally do.

**Cardamom Pods (White)**: These are green pods that have undergone chemical processing that turns them white and reduces the flavor. White cardamom is seldom used in Indian food and the whole pods are rare, but it is frequently seen as the bottled ground spice. It is only good for desserts and exotic cocktails.

**Cinnamon**: I included this seemingly common ingredient in the list because the cinnamon used in traditional Indian cuisine is not the same as the cinnamon used in western cooking, which is actually cassia. "True cinnamon", as it is often called, is only found in Indian specialty stores or online.

**Curry Leaves**: If only the fresh leaves were available—but they almost never are outside of southeast Asia. They lose their aroma and flavor within a couple of days of being picked. I almost never bother with the dried product because it has so little flavor as to be almost worthless. Curry Leaves are used extensively in the cooking of southern India, but thankfully not as important in northern India, which is generally the more popular style among westerners.

**Fenugreek**: Both the seeds and the dried leaves are used, and are quite different from each other. The leaves are can be compared to a cross between parsley and chervil. The seeds have an aroma of wheat toast and maple syrup. Like Lovage, Fenugreek is also mysteriously absent from modern western cuisine, despite it being ancient and commonplace in other parts of the world. This is especially peculiar considering that it has been medically shown to increase natural breast growth in women, as well as having been clinically used to control diabetes, and it even reduces the risk of certain types of cancer. You would think that it would be immensely popular as a dietary supplement, if nothing else. Yet somehow it hasn't caught on. The seeds should always be toasted by themselves because they burn easily and go from being fragrant and pleasant to acrid and bitter very quickly.

**Kapok Buds**: Also known as Marathi Moggu. These are the unopened buds of the Red Silk Tree. They resemble capers and are sometimes even mislabeled as "Indian Capers", but they are unrelated and completely different in taste. Like Dagarful (Black Stone Flower), Kapok Buds are primarily used in the unique Chettinad cuisine of South India. Both are available from specialty Internet spice merchants. Chettinad is in Tamil Nadu, at the far south of India. They have a history in banking and finance, which is probably why their cuisine is less vegetarian and more protein-oriented than most of India—and the only place I know in India where lobster is common. Chettinad cuisine is primarily chicken and seafood dishes, as they do not consume either beef or pork.

**Mace**: Very similar to nutmeg because it comes from the surrounding blades of the same nutmeg fruit. However, like ajwain, the component oils in mace are volatile so this should be added at the end of cooking. Ideally you will purchase mace as the dried blades and grind them yourself just before using, but in many parts of the world the pre-ground spice is all you can get. In that case, label the bottle with the date you purchased it.

**Mustard Oil**: This can range in potency from sinus-clearing (think Chinese hot mustard) to mild, depending on the amount of processing and the age. Most Indians use Mustard Oil to sauté foods in, and the heat of the pan mellows out the potency. Western chefs have discovered this ingredient recently, and they tend to use it in cold dressings, marinades and pickling. There are also Indian pickles that employ both mustard oil and mustard seeds, too. Because it was recently determined to be mildly carcinogenic, the United States and some other nations banned Mustard Oil from being labeled as an ingredient for cooking. This didn't seem to affect the actual use, though (restaurants still use it freely). You can find Mustard Oil for sale as a massage oil in many organic and health food stores, as well as in specialty Asian markets and online.

**Mustard Seeds**: There are three distinctive types of Mustard Seeds used around the world: Black, Brown, and the so-called White (which is actually yellow). The rule is that the darker the seed, the more complex and intensely flavored it is. One of the secrets of quality Indian restaurant cooking is black mustard seeds, which are the traditional type. However, these days brown mustard seeds (sometimes called "Indian Mustard") are far more prevalent because of lower cost since they can be harvested by machine, while the black type of seed requires laborious manual picking. When toasting mustard seeds, you must take care not to let them burn, as they become especially acrid. There is also a bright yellow variety of seed that is known as "hot mustard". This is what's used to make Chinese hot mustard (the condiment) as well as being the key ingredient in many Wasabi pastes. Incidentally, American mustard (the condiment) usually contains a high ratio of turmeric.

**Nigella, or Charmushka, or Black Cumin, etc.**: This is another spice that is frequently mislabeled and confused with other unrelated spices. The correct name is nigella, but it is very often called black cumin and (in the USA) sometimes called charnushka, and also mislabeled as black onion seeds. Botanically it is not related to either cumin or onion. This confusion is made even worse by the existence of another rather obscure spice in northern India that actually is called black cumin (kala jeera). Just when you thought it couldn't get any more confused, it is often called shah jeera in Indian recipes, which is spelled nearly the same as shahi jeera, or caraway—but it is nothing like caraway, either. The seeds have very little aroma compared to the massive taste that they pack. They must be used sparingly because even a little can overwhelm a dish. The flavor is unique and any attempt to describe it by comparisons to other spices would only be misleading. It is like trying to describe the sound of a particular symphony.

**Pomegranate Seeds**: The semi-dried seeds of pomegranate, are called Anardana, are used in both Indian and Middle Eastern cooking. Long ago this was mostly used in Gujarati cuisine, but interest in that region's cuisine spread across India because Gandhi was from that westernmost state. Gujarati cuisine is strictly vegetarian and typically combines sweet fruit flavors with very hot spices. Pomegranate is a popular source of tart sweetness.

**Poppy Seeds**: While these are sometimes put on breads and other baked goods in western countries, I have included poppy seeds here because they play a different role in Indian cooking. Poppy seeds are a key ingredient in Bengali and Mughlai cuisines. Aside from their delicate nutty flavor, they are also used as a thickening agent. A special white species of poppy is grown and sold in bottles as a paste for thickening light-colored dishes, mostly being Mughlai. Although opium is made from poppies, it is virtually absent in food products—at least when it comes to the narcotic effects. However consuming poppy seeds is a well documented way to fail a drug test, just so you know—especially with Indian food that may contain the aforementioned concentrated paste.

**Pudina**: Also known as wild mint. This seems to be especially common in the cuisine of central India (*e.g.* Hyderabad). It is used both in the fresh and the dried forms. Substitute ordinary fresh or dried mint, accordingly.

**Sumac**: This is a member of the cashew family and has a lemon-like sour taste. It's called Kankrasing in Hindi. I didn't include it in the chart above because it is seldom used in India these days, having been largely replaced by Amchoor (page 35) and Citric Acid (page 44). However, Sumac remains popular in the Middle East and it does occasionally show up in Indian daal and lentil recipes. The best grade is made from carefully seeded dried fruit of *Rhus coriaria*, unfortunately that best grade is very difficult to find. The Sumac that is generally available contains ground seeds from the plant, and it is unpleasantly gritty. In a sauce (or curry) that will be passed through a sieve, this isn't a problem—although you may need to pass it through the sieve two or three times.

**Tamarind**: This fruit gets its sourness from tartaric acid, which is also strongly present in red wine. Tamarind is rich in minerals, which is why it has a metallic taste when consumed on its own. Most Indian cookery involves reconstituting dried tamarind with hot water, but the paste in jars is often much better quality.

**Turmeric**: Ubiquitous ingredient of curries, and especially in large amounts in south India for vegetarian dishes. Also see pages 41-42 on turmeric in the original British curry powders.

# TOASTING SPICES

Spices may be dry roasted, cooked in oil (also called frying the spices, and sometimes called blooming), or boiled in water. Each of these methods produces different results, and you might not need to toast them at all if you are going to use them in a dry rub on meat that will be pan fried, because the spices will toast directly on the meat, and the moisture and fat from the meat will protect them from burning as long as aren't blackening the meat - and blackening can be a technique on its own where you actually do want to burn the spices some, but that's another topic. Blackening is not toasting.

Every spice used in cooking contains multiple chemical components that come together to produce the aroma and flavor that we associate with that spice (see pages 15-20). They have different boiling points (the temperature at which they leave the spice and move into the surrounding medium (air, oil or water, depending on what method you are using). Each has a different solubilitiy in oil vs. water, so if you heat the spice up in oil, a lot of the water-soluble flavors will evaporate, which obviously changes the overall flavor. In the same way, if you boil a spice, some of the oil-soluble components are driven off. Again, the flavor is changed.

So what about dry roasting? The poetic answer that you usually hear is toasting "wakes up the flavors", but this has nothing to do with reality. Chemicals don't sleep, so they can't be woken up,. The real answer is that spices were all living plant matter at one time. On a microscopic level there are still cells, even though they dead and dried. Oils are trapped inside of those cells. When you heat them up enough, the cells rupture, releasing the flavor components. Grinding also does this, but on a microscopic level, ground spices that have not been toasted still have the majority of the cells intact, with the flavor components locked away in the cells. Grinding ruptures some cells, coating the outside with the volatile flavor components, which is why ground spices lose their flavor sooner.

Where you have to be especially careful is toasting ground spices. This is almost impossible to accomplish dry without some burning. Pre-ground spices are rarely preferable to freshly ground spices. The exception are spices that are very difficult to grind yourself to a perfectly fine powder, such as cinnamon and turmeric.

When it comes to toasting, ground spices are the single easiest way to have your dish taste burnt. The safest way to do it is to heat up oil and then pour the hot oil over the ground spices in a bowl, mixing them together. Conversely, this method is not very effective with large whole spices like cinnamon, where hot oil won't do much.

Let toasted spices cool before grinding, or the volatile oils will blast away from the residual heat.

## Oven Roasting Spices

The British invention of curry powder did something that Indians probably never experienced, because they don't use low-temperature ovens traditionally. Indians use very hot tandoor ovens, open fires, and stove top burners. By roasting spices at a low temperature for hours, a different flavor profile is obtained. This is akin to what I wrote about in this book under *Ground Dried Vegetables and Fruits as Seasonings* (page 22). This is a process normally used in factory manufactured foods, but alien to traditional Indian cuisine, which is probably the biggest reason why curry powder has always been regarded with disdain by Indians (*i.e.* it is quite different in taste from what they are used to). It is like trying to tell an Italian that ketchup makes a good pasta sauce. But that's not to say that ketchup isn't a useful and interesting tomato product in its own right. You just won't find many Italians using ketchup on anything, just as you won't find Indians using curry powder (at least not in home kitchens in India).

## The Original British Curry Powder Blends

What has been mostly forgotten in culinary history books now is that originally there was not one generic "curry powder". There were many different types, each tailored to a specific Indian dish (or anglicized version of an Indian dish, I should really say). The makers tried to include all of the ingredients that the British would have a hard time procuring, which was almost everything used in Indian food at that time. English kitchens could not be relied upon to have garlic, ginger or cilantro back then, so all of these components had to be included in the mix, which was accomplished by drying and powdering them. The results were fairly good, but far better results are obtained by using fresh aromatics and herbs as I have done in my versions of those early recipes here on pages 126 and 128.

## Turmeric in British Curry Powders

What's especially interesting is how much turmeric was used in these British interpretations. I don't know of any authentic Indian spice blend with such a high percentage of turmeric, and yet the results are very good this way. The reason is probably not obvious to most people: The turmeric functions mostly as an absorbant. When the spices are roasted slowly, the oils that come out of them are trapped in the fine particles of the turmeric, where they are preserved until the actual dish is cooked. The genius of this is that at the same time, the potency of the turmeric is reduced due to the prolonged roasting. So the large volume of turmeric isn't a problem.

The only thing I have significantly changed is that the original curry powder recipe called for freshly dried and powdered turmeric roots. Fresh turmeric is hard to find, and even more difficult to dry and powder yourself at home. I'll warn you that it can easily break an electric spice mill. It is a laborious task with a marble mortar and pestle. The results are only slightly better than high quality fresh bottled powdered turmeric. Considering the difficulty, I suggest sticking to a first rate commercially dried and ground product.

## Dry Toasting vs. Frying Spices in Oil

Dry toasting spices takes place at a much higher temperature than frying them in oil. Plus, the volatile compounds go off into the air when dry toasting. If you fry them, the oil controls the heat and traps some of the volatile flavor components. In short, the difference is that dry toasting will produce a darker and earthier flavor, while frying gives more of the original brighter characteristic notes. The biggest problem with fried spices is that an electric spice mill won't work on them. Grit and tooth-crunching nuggets will be left in the final dish if you aren't passing the sauce through a sieve. The solution in India is a long time spent grinding by hand.

# ADVICE FROM
# PAUL PRUDHOMME

In my opinion, too much emphasis has been placed on knife technique when judging the abilities of a chef. I've seen prep cooks who were like human food processors but couldn't even boil pasta properly, and I've seen old grandmothers who couldn't cut a straight line in a stick of butter, but could make wonderfully delicious meals.

There is a practical and an artistic side to knife skills. Dicing vegetables into uniform sizes will ensure that they all cook at the same rate, which is often very important in the refined cuisines of Europe. So much so that it goes without ever being questioned by most cooks. This idea is not always valid, though.

Many years ago I spent a little time with Paul Prudhomme, Louisiana's legend of Creole cooking. One important idea that I took away from that experience was that the traditional approach to evenly cutting vegetables is often detrimental to the final product, especially when making sauces. To get layers of flavor, you want pieces of vegetables that have been cooked to different amounts. Some small bits that are almost burned and some larger pieces that are barely cooked. Blending these together will produce a much more complex flavor.

I'll often cut the same vegetable into two, three or four sizes. Especially when it is going to be puréed later anyway. Especially onions, bell pepper and celery—the so called "trinity" of Cajun and Creole cuisine. I don't show this in videos because I would have to explain why each time and argue with people in the comments.

Before you waste time making sure that every cube of vegetable is perfectly evenly cut, consider how visible it is going to be in the final dish. If it is going to be cooked until it is soft and mushy, then it won't make any difference and the flavor may well benefit from some variation. This isn't a license to be sloppy, though. You have to make conscious choices about what you are doing.

# CITRIC ACID & SODIUM CITRATE

Although it has a citrus taste, Citric Acid is not at all the same as lemon because all of the other chemical components that create the flavor we regard as "lemon" are missing—which is about a third of the flavor in a lemon (2/3 being citric acid). Commercially, citric acid is widely used in place of lemon juice because it is cheap and it won't spoil, but it is not a quality substitute. Citric acid should be regarded as a separate ingredient and not a substitute for lemon.

Citric Acid is often labeled as "sour salt" in stores. Sodium Citrate is confusingly also labeled as "sour salt", particulary in Jewish kosher stores. To convert Citric Acid to Sodium Citrate, you can use a simple chemical reaction. For every 100 grams of Citric Acid, mix 43 grams of Sodium Bicarbonate, then add water. There will be a LOT of foaming! When the foaming stops, dry it in the oven at 80°C (150°F) and then crush the solids to make a powder.

## Citric Acid and GMO Concerns

There is some Internet scare mongering about citric acid and GMO's, but citric acid is a pure chemical. It doesn't make any difference where it came from originally. An analogy would be the gasoline you put in your car. It doesn't matter whether it came from oil out of Texas or out of Saudi Arabia. After it has been refined and processed, it is all the same. How citric acid was produced is irrelevant by the time it is in crystalline pure state. I'm not going to take sides in the GMO debate because it is more complex than people can understand without an actual education in biochemistry. I will say that I find it ironic that people are so concerned about that particular source of contamination. What you should really be concerned about is your air, because that's the greatest amount of chemical and biological contamination in your life. Each person breathes in about 11,000 liters of air in a single day.

## Sodium Citrate in Cheese Sauces

Sodium Citrate (not citric acid) is used commercially to make liquid cheese sauces. It is also the secret behind Swiss Fondue, although in that case it is added in the form of a wine that has been selected for having Sodium Citrate in it naturally (along with some other acid salts that function in a similar way). A little known fact is that making fondue with the wrong wine will never produce results. Nacho cheese sauce and Kraft's Macaroni and Cheese are also examples of how Sodium Citrate keeps cheese in a liquid state.

## Citric Acid in Dry Rubs

This is an outstanding ingredient for dry rubs used on poultry, fish and sometimes lamb, but generally not advisable for beef or pork. Remember that it is acidic and should not be used in reactive metal cookware. Like dried herbs, some care must be taken not to burn Citric Acid, as it decomposes at 175°C (350°F).

On hearing this, you might think that it would burn in any oven set above 175°C (350°F), but oven temperature is not the same thing. Seasonings that are in contact with meat or vegetables are protected from burning by surface moisture. The exceptions to this are when you are cooking on a very hot grill or over an open fire. Now you have introduced so much heat that herbs and certain other flavorings such as Citric Acid and MSG will actually burn because moisture is being driven off of the surface faster than it can escape from inside the food.

Aside from carbon dioxide and water, Citric Acid decomposes into Aconitic Acid (an acidic taste), Citraconic Acid (a unique and unpleasant odor) and Acetonedicarboxylic Acid (smells like nail polish remover). Therefore, it is not recommended to use Citric Acid on foods that will be grilled over coals or fire. *Indirect* heat is fine.

## Citric Acid vs. Cream of Tartar

Although Cream of Tartar (chemically Potassium Hydrogen Tartrate) is also a powdered acidic component used in cooking, it is completely different in both taste and chemical properties. It is less acidic and far less soluble. One reason why it is used to beat egg whites is because it doesn't dissolve easily and the little crystals help break up the albumen as the blades whip through it. Some old fashioned recipes mistakingly call for Cream of Tartar where lemon juice should be used. See my pancake recipe (page 54).

# MICROWAVE OVEN PHYSICS

There is an alarming amount of erroneous information on this topic, including some from otherwise reputable sources—to say nothing of the utter nonsense from hacks and quacks.

In order to correctly view the nature of microwave heating, you must first consider how we define and measure temperature itself. Conventional heating of any liquid involves the *translational* motion of molecules. That's the scientific term for objects moving around in three-dimensional space. If you walk across the room, you have engaged in translational motion—as opposed to vibrational or rotational motion. Touch your toes a few times without walking anywhere and you have performed the equivalent of vibrational motion. Spin around in one place and you have engaged in rotational motion. Thermometers are not affected very much by either of the latter two types of kinetic energy. Thermometers measure translational motion. Normally that's just fine because when we heat something up there is an equal distribution of translational, vibrational and rotational movements, so the fact that we are only measuring one type of energy is irrelevant—and it doesn't matter if the solution was heated over an open fire, or in an oven, or just left out in the sunlight—a thermometer will provide an accurate measurement of what we normally define as temperature.

In conventional heating there is a finite limit to the amount of energy that a liquid can absorb before it reaches its boiling point. The molecules are colliding with each other at such a furious rate that some break through the surface tension and escape into the atmosphere. You can think of this like a room full of blindfolded people running around and bumping into each other. Each person can only run so fast or so far before they collide with someone else, which slows them down again. Occasionally someone gets pushed out of a window or a doorway, but most of the crowd remains trapped inside.

However, microwave heating works in an entirely different and unnatural way. To use the same analogy, the people in the room are spinning around. There is almost no limit as to how fast something can spin in place, if you think about it. The limitation imposed by collisions has been minimized. Of course some do collide with the surrounding non-water molecules and transfer kinetic energy in the form of translational energy, which is how microwave ovens work, but the heating is highly uneven. There are local pockets of water with more kinetic energy than they ever could have accumulated by conventional heating—all rotational, of course. We don't even have a way of describing this sort of "temperature" in our language, or any sort of thermometer that can measure it. It doesn't happen in nature.

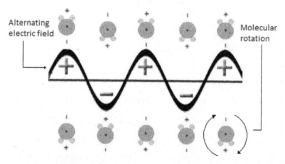

Water molecules can continue to accelerate as they are under the influence of the microwave field to rather fantastic energy levels. If we were to mathematically convert their rotational kinetic energy into translational energy, we would find the localized regions where the temperature is hundreds of degrees above the boiling point! Yet the solution does not boil because there is so little translational energy. This is why if you heat up a glass of water for a long time in a microwave and then touch the surface with something, it can explode in a geyser of superheated steam.

As long as you are heating water by itself, there is nothing for it to react with (water doesn't react with itself). But when you microwave foods, you have created a situation in which water molecules have enough energy to cause chemical reactions that transform safe organic molecules into carcinogens. The longer you microwave something, the greater the concentration of carcinogens that can build up. A few seconds to warm up a plate of food is one thing, but five minutes or more is quite another. In fact, one of the newest areas of organic lab chemistry is the use of microwave ovens to perform organic syntheses—with carcinogens as proven and expected by-products. The entire industry of frozen microwave foods relies on this remaining misunderstood by the public.

# SMOKING FOODS

There are three approaches to the direct use of burning wood...

**TRADITIONAL SMOKER**

Burning wood creates nitric oxide gas that chemically reacts with myoglobin in the meat. This is what creates the "smoke ring" that is visible in sliced smoked meats. As you can also see, the penetration of the effect is still limited to a few millimeters. The pros are that the smoke is intense and has actually integrated with the meat itself. The cons are that it requires a lot of time, special equipment and produces highly variable results in the hands of amateurs.

**STOVE TOP SMOKER**

The main problem with this device is that you are limited to hot smoking, and the smoke tends to be very intense— although you can control that some by using only a tiny quantity of wood chips. Still, you are cooking the food at a fairly high temperature at the same time you are smoking it, which means you have two different operations going on that must be synchronized.

**SMOKING GUN**

This relatively new technology involves a piece of equipment that is rather like a tobacco pipe connected to an electric air pump. Wood chips burn in the pipe and smoke blows out of a flexible hose. Foods to be smoked are placed in a closed container that is filled with smoke from the hose. There is no heat, so the smoke molecules simply stick to the moist surface of the meat. The pros are that it is convenient and fast, and since it does not introduce any heat, it can be used on anything from fruit to sushi. The cons are that it requires fairly expensive special equipment and (more important) since the smoke is limited to what can adhere to the surface, the effect is mild by comparison to other methods.

Aside from the use of actual smoke directly, there are a couple of other ways of delivering smoky goodness to foods. The most important of these is ***Liquid Smoke**. Most people are unaware that this has became almost the universal method in commercially "smoked" packaged foods for two reasons: First, because it can be easily and accurately controlled for consistent results. Second—and this surprises nearly everyone—because liquid smoke does not contain polycyclic hydrocarbons, so it is <u>less</u> carcinogenic!

Your only other option for introducing a smoky flavor is a smoked salt or spice (such as smoked paprika). While it is not a replacement for any of these other methods because the smokiness is subtle, this is an option to keep in mind. The smoked salt by Maldon is nice for the large flake size that helps it stick to things like roasted chicken, but it is not as smoky as some other brands. I'm especially fond of the black alder smoked salt offered by Epicure Selections (epicureselections.com). Also very worthwhile—though expensive—is the oak smoked product, Halen Môn Gold Smoked Sea Salt available online from The Meadow (atthemeadow.com), as pictured above on the right. The Meadow also offers some other smoked salts, but they are not as good.

* For more about liquid smoke, see "The Chemistry of Smoked Foods", by Gilbert and Knowles in the *International Journal of Food Science & Technology* (June, 1975; Vol. 10, No. 3, pgs. 245–261).

# KITCHEN GADGETS

Some *must-have* items for any serious cook...

### Ceramic Spice Mill

After just mentioning smoked salt (previous page), I must tell you to get a high quality ceramic spice mill. One example of this is Kyocera's *Everything Mill*. These enable you to grind spices (and smoked salt) directly onto food in a controlled amount. They are similar to pepper mills, but not the same. A pepper mill will not work on much else but pepper, but a ceramic spice mill will work on almost anything (though ironically not especially well on peppercorns). I keep six of these loaded with the following: Welsh alder smoked salt, Spanish saffron salt, Italian black truffle salt, coriander seeds, cumin seeds, and caraway.

### Electric Spice Mill

These are usually sold with the intention of them being used as an electric coffee grinder. Anyone who has watched my videos on YouTube knows that I use this device constantly, but what I have not bothered to explain is the benefit that it has for grinding up dried herbs and even spices that are already ground. All of these things were plants originally, and on a microscopic level they still have cell membranes. The more you tear those open, the more flavor is released. Now the flipside to that is that they will burn easier when you grind them up, so you have to consider the application. If you are going to be cooking something over a barbecue pit, you don't want ultrafine particles because they'll burn. However, the moisture that is naturally present as meat cooks is often enough to protect the seasoning from burning, providing that you are not using an extremely high temperature or taking the browning right to the edge of black.

### Garlic Peeler

This ingenius device was originally nothing more than a section of ordinary garden hose that the inventor packaged up and marketed. If you have an old hose, you can make your own and even wrap them up as presents for your friends. By placing the clove in the tube and rolling it back and forth, the skin comes off perfectly cleanly and effortlessly. Don't run the tube through the dishwasher, though. They will shrivel up, and they don't need that sort of cleaning anyway.

## Garlic Press

This is a standard piece of equipment already in most kitchens. The problem is that it is often used as a lazy way of mincing garlic. Minced garlic and crushed garlic are quite different in most applications. The more cell membranes you rupture, the more reactions take place of the air-sensitive active compounds, and this has a profound effect on both the flavor and how it cooks. When crushed garlic is called for, don't dice it, and vice versa.

Many European chefs hate the taste of garlic after it has been crushed in a garlic press, saying that it has been turned into something vile and unnatural. Never the less, there are times when this "vile" ingredient is called for, particularly in marinades.

> *To maximize the flavor, allow chopped or minced garlic to stand for several minutes before adding it to a dish or cooking vessel, because the chemical flavor component allicin will not form after it is heated or exposed to acidic ingredients. It forms in air at room temperature. This is especially true for vinaigrettes.*

## Food Mill

This is a hand-cranked device that forces a mixture through a perforated plate. Better models come with a selection of several plates with different diameter holes for different applications. They can be used to make perfectly smooth mashed potatoes that are, in turn, perfect for making gnocchi from because the potatoes are crumbled up gently (a ricer can also be used for that task, but a ricer is not as generally useful as a food mill). A food mill is also indispensable for separating skin and seeds from volumes of tomatoes. See the picture on the following page.

FOOD MILL

## Fat Separating Pitcher

In a home kitchen this is an indispensable piece of equipment. Without it you will either fail to skim fat cleanly, or be forced to wait for overnight refrigeration to solidify the fat layer so that it can be removed as a solid. The price of this gadget is so low that there is no excuse for not owning one.

FAT SEPARATING PITCHER

# Russian Recipes

As I explained in detail in Volume 1, there is no true Russian cuisine. Every dish was imported from the surrounding regions, or brought in by a visiting foreign chef from Europe. For more about the complex history of Russian cuisine (or rather the lack thereof), see Volume 1 of this cookbook series. So, while these dishes are known in various parts of Russia today, they had their origin in either the surrounding former republics, or were invented by visiting European chefs.

## The Coal Miner's Breakfast and Russian Cuisine

One of the most grueling and life-shortening jobs in American history was that of a coal miner in the 19th Century. The life expectancy of a worker was only about two years, after which point the person would be such a wreck that they could no longer perform the job. They would typically consume only one meal a day—breakfast. That meal would be unfathomably rich, with 10,000 calories or more. Yet the workers were still skin and bones because they would burn those calories off in the mine. A similar history in Eastern Europe existed, and Russians are still accustomed to the sort of heavy, fatty dishes that Americans were enjoying 50 years ago or more. A soup with a thick layer of grease from animal fat floating on top is a delight to many, particularly those in the Caucas regions. Something low in calories is generally seen as food for little girls, or a restaurant ripping them off.

Most of my recipes have been tailored to the tastes of Russians over the years. "Light and healthy" is rarely part of the vocabulary. Neither is "gluten free". This is more like America, circa 1950.

# BLINI AND OLADJI
# (PANCAKES)

*While blini are the most well known style of pancake in Russia, they were born of poverty, being made mostly with water instead of eggs and milk. The Russian fast food chain Teremok that specializes in blini has capitalized on the low cost of this food product. Oladji are similar to American pancakes, but made without baking powder. I combined elements of all three styles of pancakes to create what I consider the absolute best—light and fluffy with no gumminess. There are two alternative versions provided, as explained below.*

| | |
|---|---|
| 240g (8.5 oz) | Flour, all purpose (see more on this below) |
| 240ml (8.5 oz) | Milk |
| 90g (3.2 oz) | Yogurt, full fat |
| 2 whole | Eggs |
| 2 T | Sugar |
| 1 t | Baking Soda |
| 1/2 t | Vanilla Extract, or 1 t Russian Vanilla Powder |
| 1/2 t | Salt |
| 30ml (1 oz) | Lemon Juice |

## BAKING SODA

Baking powder is still unavailable in Russia even now as of the time of writing this. Baking soda is the chemical sodium bicarbonate. Mixing baking soda with vinegar or lemon juice causes a chemical reaction that releases carbon dioxide gas. The effect is quite different from baking powder, where the gas is released mostly upon heating. The baking soda and lemon juice mixture is a well known baking trick in Russia.

## ADDITIONAL TIPS

The ideal way to cook these is on an electric griddle that has a thermostat to regulate the temperature. Of course you can cook these on a nonstick pan on the stove, too.

To turn this into blini batter, after the batter has rested for 15-20 minutes, whisk in water, as explained in the procedure below. Although different from French crepes, these blini are good for filling with either savory or sweet ingredients.

## PROCEDURE

1. Whisk together all of the ingredients except the lemon juice.
2. Add the lemon juice and whisk to combine.
3. Allow to stand undisturbed at room temperature for 15-20 minutes.
4. If making blini, now whisk in 200ml (7 ounces) water.
5. On a hot nonstick skillet or griddle, add either butter (for pancakes / oladji) or brush with vegetable oil for blini. Ladle batter out.
6. Cook until 2/3 done and then flip for the final third of the cooking time
7. Transfer to a platter and brush with butter.

## BUCKWHEAT VARIATION

My personal favorite modification is substituting 10% of the flour with buckwheat flour plus the addition of 15ml (1 tablespoon) of Amaretto.

You can use 100% buckwheat flour in place of the regular flour, but then double the milk to 480ml (17 oz). The batter will need more whisking than with regular flour. Fry these in a mixture of butter and oil. Use a slightly lower heat setting and allow longer to cook. Even if you thought you didn't like buckwheat, this will very likely change your mind—and buckwheat is healthier. They are even lighter and flakier than the pancakes made with wheat flour, but they are more difficult to cook well.

# CHICKEN FRANCAISE

*These days most people don't think of this as a Russian recipe, but according to culinary history, it dates to 18th Century Moscow when it was the invention of a visiting French chef. For more about this era, see the section on Russian culinary history in Volume 1.*

| | |
|---|---|
| 2 | Chicken Breasts, boneless and skinless |
| 2 t | French Herbs from Lyon (page 194) |
| 45 g (1.5 oz) | Butter |
| 1 clove | Garlic, crushed with the side of a knife |
| 1 T | Lemon Juice, fresh |
| 1/4 t | White Pepper, ground |
| 1/4 t | Mustard, dry |
| 2 | Egg Yolks |

## FRENCH HERBS

The key to the success of this recipe is the blend of herbs. This is the sort of detail that is often overlooked. Many cooks, especially home cooks in Russia, use bottles of premixed "French herbs" for everything. There is no such thing as a one-size-fits-all blend. The herbs used here are most of the flavor in this dish. In this case I am using a blend that's typical of Lyon, which is where the original chef who served this in Russia was from. Although I always say that there is no such thing as a perfect dish, I can't imagine improving on this version.

## ADDITIONAL TIPS

Serve additional sauce on the side in either a small gravy boat, or a ramekin for dipping. Steamed vegetables on the side are highly recommended.

## PROCEDURE

1. Trim the chicken breasts to remove the strip known as the "tender" and the heavy ligament fiber that runs along it. Now sandwich the breast between layers of plastic cling film and pound until it is uniformly 1 centimeter thick (about 0.4 inches). For a restaurant application, we would further trim the edges to make it a nice even shape, but you lose a lot of meat this way, and it is purely for aesthetics. Your decision.

2. Divide the French herbs between the two flattened breasts on both sides. Then sprinkle with salt and a little white pepper on one side.

3. Heat the butter in a large good quality heavy nonstick skillet until it comes to 95°C (200°F). Add the garlic clove and dry mustard. Adjust heat to medium-low (#4 out of 10). Put the two chicken breast pieces in. Begin counting the time. Cook for 4 minutes. Maintain the temperature and don't let it climb much above 100°C (210°F).

4. Turn the chicken breasts over and cook for another 3 minutes.

5. Remove the chicken to a platter to keep warm. Remove the garlic and discard.

6. While whisking the egg yolks in a bowl, slowly and carefully pour the melted butter and pan juices in. The residual heat from the hot butter will cook the egg yolks sufficiently. Now add the lemon juice and whisk more. Pass through a sieve, if desired. This will produce a nicer looking sauce, but it isn't really necessary.

7. Put some of the sauce down on the plates with the chicken on top. A sprig of parsley is a common garnish, as well as some glazed vegetables such as carrots, zucchini and/or broccoli.

# OLIVIER SALAD

*The term "salad" is generally taken to mean a cold vegetable dish of some type. The type of salad Americans think of is referred to as "greens". Many Russian salads are some mixture of vegetables bound with mayonnaise, but Olivier is the most famous of all—and to make it well requires time and patience.*

| | |
|---|---|
| 270g (9.5 oz) | Potatoes, waxy type - cubed small |
| 90g (3.2 oz) | Carrot, cubed small |
| 60gj (2.1 oz) | Celery Root, cubed small |
| 80g (2.8 oz) | Sausage, cubed small (see notes below) |
| 60g (2 oz) | Smoked Duck, cubed small |
| 60g (2 oz) | Crawfish Tails, boiled |
| 50g (1.8 oz) | Cauliflower, roasted with spices (see below) |
| 30g (1 oz) | Peas, either frozen or canned |
| 30g (1 oz) | Dill Pickles, cubed small |
| 1-2 T | Scallions, finely minced |
| 2 | Eggs, hard boiled |
| 1/2 t | MSG |
| 150g (5 oz) | Mayonnaise, or Dressing (see note below) |

## THE SAUSAGE

Russian Валенсия (Valencia) sausage is my choice for this, but that variety is difficult to find outside of Russia, except sometimes in specialty Russian stores. Substitute an Italian mild cured smoked pork sausage, Avoid cheap cuts like sandwich bologna.

## THE PEAS

Almost every Russian uses canned peas for this. The distinctive taste is part of what they remember from their childhood. If you are making this for Russians, follow that tradition. Otherwise you will enjoy this more with frozen peas that are blanched, as explained in the procedure.

## THE DRESSING

As with the canned peas, Russians grow up expecting a certain familiar taste, which is a pure mayonnaise dressing. This is not what Oliver became famous for. The recipe that follows is a dressing that is far more interesting, but Russians are happy with commercial mayonnaise

## ROASTED SEASONED CAULIFLOWER (OPTIONAL)

This is an additional step to increase the depth of the flavor. It's the sort of thing that is done in a fine restaurant, but not by home cooks in Russia. You can simply omit the cauliflower and skip to step 4 below.

| | |
|---|---|
| 90-120g (4 oz) | Cauliflower (see notes) |
| 22ml (3/4 oz) | Vegetable Oil, ideally unfiltered Sunflower |
| 22ml (3/4 oz) | Balsamic Vinegar |
| 3/4 t | Coriander Seeds |
| 3/4 t | Garlic Powder |
| 3/4 t | Salt |
| 1/2 t | Black Peppercorns |

## PROCEDURE

1. Cut cauliflower as shown in the diagram below.

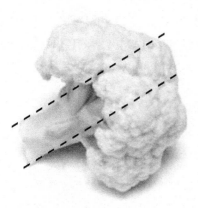

Cut the edges off of each floret of cauliflower (along the lines shown in the diagram) so that you have the center pieces with flat surfaces for this. The edge pieces you trim off can be used in soups or vegetable purées. Also see the *Lobster and Pan Roasted Vegetable Salad* (page 146).

2. Grind the spices and mix with the oil and vinegar. Toss the cauliflower pieces in the mixture to coat evenly. Let marinate for 20-30 minutes.

3. Spread the pieces out on a baking tray covered with either parchment paper or a silicone mat (Silpat) and roast at 200°C / 400°F or 30 minutes, turning the pieces over after the first 15 minutes have elapsed.

4. Refer to the video on preparing the smoked duck from confit duck legs and on how to cut the vegetables into even dice.

5. Bring a pot of salted water to a rapid boil and add the cubed potatoes. Cook for 7 minutes.

6. Skim off the potatoes and cook the celery root in the same pot of boiling water until tender.

7. Skim off the celery root, then cook the carrots in the same water.

8. If you are using frozen peas, then cook them in the same boiling water for about 3 minutes.

9. Let the vegetables cook to room temperature at least. Refrigerating them first is even better. During this time you can prepare the scallions, pickles, duck, hard boiled eggs, etc.

10. Combine all of the ingredients except for about half of the crawfish tails which you should reserve as a garnish. Stir gently with the mayonnaise so as not to pulverize the vegetables. The cut pieces of vegetable should still be recognizeable and separate pieces in the dressing. Plate with sprigs of fresh dill and the rest of the crawfish tails.

# ALTERNATE OLIVIER SALAD DRESSING

Olivier Salad is commonly called "Russian Salad" in other European nations, even though it was invented by a Belgian chef working in Russia at the time. Although his dressing was similar to mayonnaise (which is what is almost always used now), he took most of the secret recipe to his grave. This is my version which has received critical acclaim in the Russian press.

| | |
|---|---|
| 60ml | White Wine, dry |
| 15g | Scallions, finely chopped |
| 30g | Brie cheese |
| 1 t | Flour |
| 20g | Butter |
| 120ml | Milk |
| 1 | Egg Yolk |
| 1/2 t | Salt |
| 60g | Mayonnaise |

## PROCEDURE

1. Combine the white wine and scallions in a small saucepan and bring to a strong simmer. Cook until nearly dry, but not burned.

2. Remove from the heat and add the brie cheese to the pan so that it melts. Allow it to cool for about 10 minutes while you do the next steps.

3. In a separate pan, cook the flour and butter slowly on a medium heat to make a thin roux. Then whisk in the milk and cook until it thickens.

5. Temper the egg yolk with some of the hot Bechamel you just prepared.

6. Whisk in the egg yolk mixture and then the scallion and brie mixture. Combine the mayonnaise and salt. Chill and store in the refrigerator.

# SAUSAGE AND POTATOES

*This is strictly a restaurant version. As explained in the video, rye bread croutons not normally part of dacha cooking, as well as several other aspects of this recipe.*

| | |
|---|---|
| 280g (10 oz) | Potatoes, cut in 1.25cm (1/2 inch) pieces |
| | Bacon, slab (cut in cubes) |
| | Sausage, lightly smoked |
| 24 cubes | Rye Bread 2-3cm (3/4-1 inch) on each side |
| 90g (3 oz) | Vegetable Oil |
| 22g (3/4 oz) | Garlic cloves |
| | Onion, thinly sliced |
| Juniper Berries (optional) | |
| Dill, fresh | |

## PAR-COOKED POTATOES

The potatoes should be cooked in twice their volume of water with one teaspoon of salt for every 140 grams (5 oz) of potato. If you don't cook the potatoes enough, they will be chewy and raw tasting. If you cook them too much, they will be fuzzy and easily broken. For really professional results you have to work out the timing perfectly, which will take several times of making it.

## ADDITIONAL TIPS

Be sure to use a waxy type of potato for this, and not a Russet. The amount of bacon, sausage and onion is up to you. Personal tastes vary widely on this matter. Some Russians argue that the meat should only be a flavoring for the potatoes, while others will complain that the dish is "all potato and no meat", so I leave it up to you.

## PROCEDURE

1. Put potatoes, water and salt into a saucepan with a lid. Turn the heat up to maximum until it comes to a boil. Now reduce heat to medium (#5 out of 10), cover and cook for about 9 minutes. The optimum time will depend on the specific type of potato you are using.

2. Drain the potatoes and put off in a bowl to cool down to room temperature, during which time they finish cooking from the residual heat. Now you can either continue with the recipe, or refrigerate the potatoes for up to two days and complete it later.

3. Purée the vegetable oil and the garlic with a little salt. Coat the rye bread cubes with this mixture and let it soak in for a few minutes.

4. Fry the croutons on a nonstick skillet for 10-15 minutes on a medium-low to medium heat. When they start to become crisp, turn the heat down and let them cook for another 5-10 minutes. Then set aside.

5. Cook the bacon in a little oil gently until it begins to render some fat.

6. Add the sliced sausage to the pan and cook with the bacon on a medium-low heat (#3 out of 10).

7. After about 3 minutes, add the potatoes to the pan. Keep the heat low. Season with *LSD Seasoning* (page 193), or your own personal favorite seasoning mixture if you don't have that. Don't stir it too much so that the potatoes have time to develop some color on them.

8. After a few minutes, turn the potatoes over and add a little thinly sliced onion and half a dozen juniper berries.

9. After a few more minutes on a low heat, stir to move the onion to the bottom of the pan and add the rye croutons.

10. After 3-4 more minutes sprinkle on freshly chopped dill. Cover and let the dill steam for about 2 minutes. Now turn the heat up all the way for about a minute (still with the lid on).

# CAMPANELLE WITH BRAISED CABBAGE, MUSTARD AND SAGE

*This simple rustic recipe with its roots in Romanian cuisine is transformed here into a dish for a fine dining restaurant.*

| | |
|---|---|
| 500g (18 oz) | Cabbage |
| 100g (3.5 oz) | Mustard Flowers, fresh |
| | or substitute 2 T Mustard Seeds, ideally brown & yellow mixed |
| 30ml (1 oz) | Mustard Oil, or vegetable oil |
| 1 1/4 T | Monosodium Glutamate (MSG) |
| | or 2 teaspoons salt |
| Few leaves Sage, or 1 teaspooon dried | |

## CAUTION ABOUT MUSTARD FLOWERS

First, be sure there were no pesticides used on them - don't buy them from a florist. If you are foraging them yourself, be sure you have the right species. Also, some people are allergic to mustard flowers. A skin rash is the most common reaction. Consume only a small amount to test your reaction if you are uncertain about your allergies.

## ADDITIONAL TIPS

This pasta shape resembles little flowers, but it varies quite a lot from one maker to another. What is ideal for this recipe is *Genuss Pur Kelche* pasta made in Germany by 3 Glocken. Their version is like a cross between chanterelle mushrooms and orchids in the shape, and the texture works perfectly with this dish. The product is widely distributed.

The sage you dry yourself will be better in this recipe than the type you buy in a bottle. For more about this, see page 21.

# PROCEDURE

1. Remove the stem (core) of the cabbage and slice the rest coarsely. Chop the mustard flowers coarsely, too.

2. Mix cabbage with the mustard flowers (or seeds), the oil, the sage and the MSG or salt. Place into a covered ovenproof dish and braise at 170°C / 340°F for 2 1/2 hours.

3. Drain the mixture on a sieve, pressing down to get rid of as much of the liquid as possible. You should have about 250g (8.8 oz) of solids.

4. Cook the pasta in boiling salted water until al dente. Be sure to save the pasta water for use later in this recipe.

| | |
|---|---|
| 150g (5.3 oz) | Campanelle |
| 150g (5.3 oz) | Puréed Tomatoes (pasata) |
| 120g (4 oz) | Braised Cabbage (see video) |
| 2 t | Dried Plum Spice Mix (page 200) |
| 1-2 T | Parsley, fresh |
| Smetana or Creme Fraiche | |
| Dried Sage | |

5. Fry the puréed tomatoes in a tablespoon of oil along with the chopped parsley on a medium-high heat (#7 out of 10).

6. After about 5 minutes when the volume has been reduced by half, add the spice mixture to it. Cook for 1-2 minutes with stirring.

7. Add the braised cabbage and mustard mixture to the tomato mixture. Cook for another 3-4 minutes.

8. Add a ladle or two of the pasta water and stir. Add the cooked pasta, then the smetana or cream fraiche. Cook another few minutes before plating. Garnish with some crumbled sage that you dried yourself.

# UZBEKI PLOV

*Here is another classic dish that evolved over centuries and is practically never seen on any restaurant menu outside of Uzbekistan, Iran and Russia.*

| | |
|---|---|
| 1.2kg (2.75 lbs) | Lamb Leg, bone-in |
| 150g (5.3 oz) | Rice, Carnerolli or Arborio |
| 120g (4.25 oz) | Onions, sliced thin |
| 70g (2 1/2 oz) | Carrots, grated |
| 4 heads | Garlic (heads - not cloves) |
| 500ml (17 oz) | Vegetable Stock (canned is okay) |
| 1/4 t | Saffron (approximately) |
| 20g (3/4 oz) | Barberries, dried (or substitute raisins) |
| 1/2 t | Nigella (black cumin) |
| 3/4 t | Thyme, dried |
| 120g (4.25 oz) | Chickpeas, canned |
| 1 T + 2 t | Central Asian Spice Mix (page 200) |

## ADDITIONAL TIPS

Nigella (black cumin) is a key ingredient in Uzbeki cuisine, but hard to find. Look for it from online merchants. Note that there are some minor differences here from the YouTube video, but watch the video anyway.

## PROCEDURE

1. Trim excess fat from the lamb leg, then cut the meat into four large pieces. Put the meat pieces in a large bowl and toss with one tablespoon of the Uzbeki Spice mix. Add the bone from the leg in the bowl and toss to pick up any extra spices. Let marinate while you do the next step.

2. Put the chunks of lamb fat into a covered braising dish and roast at 200°C/390°F for about an hour to render liquid fat out of it.

3. Remove the braising dish from the oven and lower the temperature to 150°C/300°F. Strain the fat through a sieve. Discard solids.

4. Heat two tablespoons of the lamb fat in a large skillet (reserve the rest of the lamb fat for later in the recipe). Brown the meat and bone in the fat.

5. Transfer the meat and bone into a close-fitting covered braising dish. Slice the tops of the garlic off to expose the cloves and place them on top of the lamb pieces. Braise for 3 to 3 1/2 hours.

6. While the lamb is braising, prepare the rest of the recipe. In the pan that the lamb was browned in (don't clean it out), either add 500ml (2 cups) water plus either 20g (3/4 oz) of powdered vegetable stock or 300g (10.6 oz) of puréed vegetables (2:1:1 onion, carrot, celery). Bring to a simmer. If you are using fresh vegetables then simmer for an hour.

7. Strain the vegetable stock into a cup and add the saffron to it.

8. When the lamb is done braising, carefully remove the garlic and lamb to a plate to reserve. Wash the rice under cold water. Put in a bowl and then strain the liquid from the braising dish over the rice. Add the barberries along with the nigella (black cumin) and the thyme. Let stand.

9. Heat a 4 liter (4 quart) stockpot (not nonstick) on maximum heat (#10 out of 10). Add 25g (7/8 oz) of the lamb fat to the pan and then the onions and a little salt. Beware of splatters. Cook the onions until well browned.

10. When the onions are well browned, add the carrots and cook on high.

11. When it is just about to start to burn, add the other two teaspoons of the spice. Stir for 30 seconds and then add the rice, stock and barberry mixture. Scrape the bottom to deglaze the pan.

12. When it starts to get dry, add the vegetable stock mix and the chickpeas. Stir. Reduce heat to medium (#4), cover and bring to a boil.

13. Reduce heat to very low (#1 1/2 out of 10) and simmer for 20 minutes.

14. Add the lamb pieces on top of the rice, return the lid and cook 10 more minutes. Remove from heat, but leave the lid on. Wait 5 minutes.. To serve, reheat the garlic cloves in a microwave or carefully under a broiler.

# AZERBAIJAN BEEF & ARTICHOKE PLOV

*If there was any justice in the food world, this dish would be as famous as macaroni and cheese. Well, it already is if you are in Azerbaijan or Iran. Elsewhere it is seldom seen.*

| | |
|---|---|
| 100-120g (4 oz) | Dopplebock Beef (see note below) |
| 60g (2 oz) | Broth from the Dopplebock Beef |
| 120g (1/2 cup) | Basmati Rice |
| 100g (3 1/2 oz) | Artichoke Hearts (see note below) |
| 45g (1 1/2 oz) | Pomegranate seeds, fresh |
| 30g (1 oz) | Parmesan or Romano, grated |
| 30g (1 oz) | Shallot, chopped fine |
| 30ml (1 oz) | Lemon Juice |
| 1 T | Garlic, crushed |
| 3/4 t | Marjoram, dried |
| 3/4 t | Oregano, dried |
| 1/2 t | Black Pepper, ground |
| 2 | Egg Yolks |

## DOPPLEBOCK BEEF

I'm making this with the *Dopplebock Beef* (see page 114). Obviously this is not traditional, but the flavor works exceptionally well.

## ADDITIONAL TIPS

Use bottled artichoke hearts packed in oil or brine. If you used the marinated Italian style artichoke hearts, the flavor won't be as authentic (though still good). This dish was reverse engineered from a recipe in Azerbaijan that included marijuana as a flavoring. When it cooks directly over the fire, the marijuana burns and flavors the dish with the smoke. If you live in a part of the world where marijuana is legal and you want to try this, then mix a little in with the egg yolk, because that's the part that will create the smoke.

# PROCEDURE

1. Skim the fat from the Dopplebock Beef broth and set it aside for some other use (such as the *Dopplebock Beef Potatoes* on page 116).

2. Put the rice in a sieve and rinse it with cold water. Transfer it to a nonstick sauce pan. Add the Dopplebock Beef Broth plus 250ml (8.75 oz) of water. Bring to a boil on the highest heat setting (#10).

3. Stir and reduce the heat down to low (#3 out of 10). Cook 10 minutes. Increase the heat a bit if you need to in order to maintain a slow simmer.

4. Remove the pan from the heat. Cover and let it sit 30-40 minutes.

5. Cube up the Dopplebock Beef. In a bowl mix the rice with the beef, marjoram, oregano, black pepper, pomegranate seeds, crushed garlic, shallots, lemon juice, artichoke hearts and parmesan (or romano) cheese. At this point you can refrigerate the mixture and finish it up on demand.

6. For each **half** of the mixture, put the egg yolk in a separate mixing bowl and add about a cup of the mixture containing all of the other ingredients to it. Mix well. If you are cooking all of it at one time, then double this, of course.

7. Oil the bottom of a metal pan that can go on top of the stove as well as in the oven. Put the mixture containing the egg yolk down first in the pan. Smooth it out evenly. Now add some of the rest of the mixture on top.

8. Preheat oven to 220°C / 425°F. Put the metal pan on one of the stove burners and set the heat to medium-high (#7-8 out of 10). Cook for about 4 minutes until the aroma just starts to smell of burn slightly.

9. Cover with foil and transfer to the preheated oven. Bake for 15-20 minutes.

10. Put it back on the stove burner. Remove the foil and cook until smoke starts to pour out of it. See the video for the amount of smoke to wait for. To plate, sprinkle with a little lemon juice and add freshly chopped scallions on top.

# GRILLED PORK WITH APPLES, ROASTED PEPPERS & RUSSIAN GARLIC

*This is a dish I created for a restaurant in Russia, where it was described on the menu as Georgian because of the flavor.*

| | |
|---|---|
| 4 | Pork Chops, thick |
| 500g (17 oz) | Pale Green or Yellow Bell Peppers |
| 2 | Granny Smith Apples |
| 6 cloves | Elephant Garlic (Russian Garlic) |
| 60g (2 oz) | Duck Stock or Chicken Stock |
| 30g (1 oz) | Dried Cranberries (optional) |
| 1/2 t | Crushed Red Pepper Flakes (see below) |
| 2 T | Tkemeli Georgian Sour Red Plum Sauce |

Pistachio Nuts, crushed and Cilantro, minced (as garnish)
Unrefined Sunflower Oil, or Vegetable Oil

## RUSSIAN GARLIC

Also known as elephant garlic and marketed as a substitute for garlic that won't give you bad breath. This is a marketing ploy. It is not garlic any more than bell peppers could be used as chili peppers. However, it is an interesting ingredient in its own right, as this recipe shows.

## ADDITIONAL TIPS

In my experience, the best brand of Tkemeli is Trest B. To make this more distinctly Georgian, increase the Tkemeli and the red chili flakes.

## PROCEDURE

1. Preheat oven to 200°C / 400°F. Remove the cores from the peppers, then trim and cut in halves. Arrange on a baking tray (outside of peppers facing up) and brush with vegetable oil and salt. Roast 15-20 minutes.

2. Allow to cool to room temperature, then peel off the blistered skins. Coarsely chop into large pieces. Set aside.

3. Core and peel the apples. Cut into chunky pieces.

4. Fry the apple pieces in a single layer on a nonstick pan with about 2 tablespoons of unrefined sunflower oil (or vegetable oil, if you must) using a medium-high heat (#7). Cook about 8 minutes without stirring to get a good amount of color on one side of the apples. Stir and cook about two more minutes.

5. Coarsely chop the Russian Garlic and add that to the pan. Cook about another 5 minutes, stirring frequently.

6. Add the duck or chicken stock, cranberries (if you are using them) and red pepper flakes to taste. Also add the roasted peppers. Cook 5 minutes.

7. Adjust the salt level to taste. Remove from heat and add the Tkemeli. You can now store this mixture in the refrigerator for up to 3 days.

8. Preferably get a pork roast so that you can use a Jaccard device on the edges before you slice chops from it (same as for steak - see page 182). Also see the video for use of the Jaccard device on the cut chops. Season with coarse salt and fresh cracked black pepper. Allow to rest at room temperature for 45 minutes, then oil one side of the meat.

9. Get the grill pan very hot (about 230°C / 450°F) before introducing the pork. Adjust the heat to keep the grill pan surface temperature around 200°C / 400°F during the cooking time. About 3 1/2 minutes per side for a 2.5cm / 1 inch piece (thickness is before applying the Jaccard device to it).

10. Put the cooked pork chops in a bowl to rest so you can collect the juices. Pour the juices into a nonstick skillet. Add half of the pepper and apple mixture and cook in the juices until most of the liquid is gone. Add the pork chops on top and cover. Cook a bit more to warm the meat up. Plate by mounding the topping on the meat with pistachios and cilantro.

# KOTLETI

*Sort of a Russian hamburger without the bread. Some version of Kotleti is standard fare in every Russian home, but a good restaurant version such as this is something that few Russian home cooks know how to make. However, you will need a meat grinder, which is a standard piece of equipment in both home and restaurant kitchens across Russia.*

| | |
|---|---|
| 450g (16 oz) | Pork and Chicken (see note below) |
| 60g (2 oz) | Shallots or substitute Red Onion |
| 60g (2 oz) | Pita Bread, fresh (see note below) |
| 30ml (1 oz) | Milk or Cream |
| 1 whole | Egg |
| 1 t | Coriander Seeds |
| 1 1/2 t | Coarse Salt |
| 1 t | Garlic Powder |
| 1/2 - 3/4 t | Lovage, dried (see note below) |
| 1/2 t | Black Peppercorns |
| Vegetable Oil | |

## THE MEAT

Kotleti can be made from any meat you like. These are commonly offered as a meat dish for the "Russian business lunch" service in a restaurant, in which case the meat is a way to use up accumulated scraps. When properly made, these use a ratio of 2 parts of fairly fatty pork to 1 part of lean chicken (*i.e.* 300 grams pork and 150 grams chicken).

## LOVAGE

You can substitute equal parts of dried parsley and dried celery leaf. Still better results will be obtained with the *LSD Seasoning* explained on page (see page 193). You can also use dried dill here, which is common.

## PITA BREAD

The bread used to make these is often an overlooked factor among Russian home cooks. Although the type of Russian bread is not available elsewhere, Pita bread will work perfectly for this. It should not be stale.

## PROCEDURE

1. Grind the coriander seeds, coarse salt, garlic powder, lovage and black peppercorns in an electric spice mill.

2. Cut the pork and chicken into cubes that can be fed into the meat grinder. Sprinkle on the spice mixture and the chopped shallots. Mix well, then pass through the grinder.

3. Put the pita bread in a food processor and run it for about a minute to get a coarse crumb consistency with a small portion of slightly larger crumbs. Put this in a large bowl.

4. Whisk the egg in a small bowl. Pour half of this into the bowl with the ground up pita bread. Add the milk and mix to combine.

5. Add half of the ground meat to this bowl and mix together with your fingers, but try not to work the meat too much or it will be tough.

6. Now add the rest of the meat and the rest of the egg. Mix to combine, again taking care not to knead it too much so that it is tough.

7. Form into cutlets (kotleti) and fry in a nonstick skillet on a medium heat (#6 out of 10) on the first side until they just start to turn golden.

8. Turn then over and continue cooking slowly for about 5 minutes.

9. Add some vegetable oil to the pan and move the cutlets around so that the bottom side is coated in the oil. Continue cooking slowly until golden brown, reducing the heat if they are browning too fast.

10. Flip and finish the cooking on the first side. In all they should take roughly 20 minutes to cook and will puff up if you did everything right.

# MORE ABOUT RUSSIAN INGREDIENTS

Here is a concise guide to some of the more important products used in Russian cooking that are often confusing for non-natives.

## Unrefined Sunflower Oil

The funny thing about this is that many Russians associate it with certain inferior dishes, so there is a bias against the taste. This is unfortunate because it is delicious and usually sells at a high price in other countries as a gourmet item, but its cheap in Russia.

## Russian Garlic

This is known as Elephant Garlic in many parts of the world, and it is quite different in taste from regular garlic. See page 70.

## Russian Mustard

Prepared mustard, that is. There are many different species of mustard plants around the world and several well known varieties such as Dijon and Chinese mustard. Russian mustard is hot, but not in the Chinese horseradish-like way. The flavor is somewhat similar to a German mustard (not whole grain), but stronger.

## Salo

This is pork fat that has been cured with salt, garlic, pepper and coriander seeds. Sometimes it is also lightly smoked. Salo is often eaten on bread like butter to go with vodka, but it is also used in some cooking. There is a similar product in Italy and other parts of Europe, but it's quite uncommon in the United States.

## Tkemeli

Also known as "Georgian Ketchup", it is sold in virtually every grocery store in Russia and is commonly used by Russians. There are two types, both made from sour plums. The red type is more popular among Russians. Georgians use both types like Americans used ketchup, thus its nickname.

# Cooking in Russia

Although I do show some Russian recipes in videos, quite a few people don't seem to pay attention to the "in" in "Cooking in Russia". Regardless of the type of cuisine you are preparing, there are certain challenges that exist simply by being <u>in</u> Russia.

One of those challenges is the total absence of certain ingredients that are readily available in many other countries. Although this was improving rapidly up until about 2012, with the worsening global economy and then the embargo, things began sliding back in the other direction again.

This is especially problematic in a restaurant because all of the items on the menu should be available, but if they require ingredients that suddenly disappear from shelves, then customers will be disappointed when they try to order things that can't be cooked. Consequently, this restricts the recipes in a restaurant to those that use only ingredients that are certain to be available. In Russia, that list of "always available items" is very short. In fact, even items that are normally part of that list can still disappear without notice or explanation. Twice now I've seen periods where garlic was not available. Recently there was no cabbage for about ten days—unthinkable in Russia where cabbage is a staple food.

However, the reason for these occurrences is not an actual shortage, but rather some snag in the distribution chain. The details as to why are complicated and unrelated to this book but suffice it to say that cooking in Russia presents some unique challenges, especially for restaurant service.

# SHRIMP WITH MUSHROOMS IN A WINE AND CREAM SAUCE

*This is an old style French recipe from the days when Paul Bocuse was the undisputed king. These days heavy cream sauces are not as popular, but still every bit as delicious.*

| | |
|---|---|
| 240g (8.5 oz) | Shrimp, raw, shell-on (see note below) |
| 240g (8.5 oz) | Mushrooms |
| 250ml (8.8 oz) | White Wine, dry |
| 130ml (4.5 oz) | Madeira (see video) |
| 65g (2.3 oz) | Shallots, diced |
| 1 clove | Garlic, coarsely chopped |
| 1 | Bay Leaf |
| 3/4 t | White Pepper, ground |
| 3/4 t | Mustard, dry |
| 1/2 t | Tarragon, dried |
| 1/16 t (pinch) | Nutmeg, ground |
| 300ml (10.6 oz) | Milk, or a mix of milk and cream if you prefer |
| 45ml (1 oz) | Olive Oil (in all) |
| 45g (1 oz) | Butter (in all) |
| 2 T | Flour |
| 1 | Egg Yolk |
| 1 T | Lemon Juice, fresh |
| 1/2 t | MSG (optional) |
| Dried Parsley flakes (garnish) | |

## RAW SHRIMP

Use shrimp about the size of an adult's pinky finger. Buy them raw with the shells on. They are easy to peel and cost less. Plus the shells are needed to make stock from, as is the case here. All seafood (shrimp, scallops, lobster, etc.) is all muscle and no fat, which means they will be rubbery if overcooked. To make matters worse, packaged shrimp that are cooked have been boiled, which is rarely ideal for a recipe.

## PROCEDURE

1. Peel and devein the shrimp. Keep the shrimp cold while you continue.

2. Heat a nonstick skillet. Add the olive oil and sauté the shrimp shells on a high heat (#8 out of 10).

3. After 3-4 minutes when fragrant, add the shallots, bay leaf and garlic.

4. After another 3 minutes add the white wine. Reduced until nearly dry.

5. Add about 90ml (3 oz) water to help transfer the contents to the cup of a stick blender. Purée until smooth, then rub through a sieve. Discard the solids and add the MSG to the shrimp stock you just strained. Set aside.

6. Dry the shrimp off. Season with salt and pepper, then fry on a very hot cast iron pan in batches. Leave them just slightly undercooked (see video).

7. Separate the stems from the caps of the mushrooms. Save the stems for the next step. If the mushrooms are large, cut the caps into halves or quarters. You want them to be about the same size as the shrimp in the finished dish, and remember that mushrooms will shrink during cooking. Put in a bowl and mix well with the lemon juice. Set aside.

8. Coarsely chop the stems and cook in a saucepan with 30g (1 oz) butter.

9. When the stems are browned, lower the heat (#2) and stir in the flour.

10. After 5 minutes with frequent stirring, add the milk, white pepper, dry mustard and tarragon. Increase the heat to medium and bring to a simmer. Stir to make a sort of mushroom Bechamel.

11. After 3-4 minutes of simmering, add 100ml (3.5 oz) of the Madeira and reduce the heat slightly (#3). Cook at a slow simmer until it thickens up again (about 7-8 minutes).

12. Taste and adjust the salt (about 1 1/2 teaspoons). It should be slightly salty because the mushrooms will be added to it, and they won't be salted. If you are unsure if you have reduced it enough, weigh it. Aim for 240 grams (8.5 oz) - about the same weight as the raw shrimp at the start.

13. First whisk in the cooled shrimp stock you prepared earlier (this will lower the temperature down) and then the egg yolk. Set aside.

14. Heat a large nonstick skillet. Add the remaining 15g (1/2 oz) butter and the same quanity of olive oil. Brown the mushroom caps.

15. Now reduce the heat to low (#3 out of 10) and add the sauce. Cook gently with stirring to thicken it up to the point of coating the back of a spoon as the egg yolk cooks.

16. Add the rest of the Madeira and the pinch of nutmeg. Cook with stirring until it starts to become thick again.

17. Remove from the heat. Transfer to a bowl and stir in the shrimp you cooked earlier. You can hold everything at this point for up to two days in the refrigerator if you need to. The only difference is that it will take a little longer to finish under the broiler in step #19 below.

18. Spoon into ramekins for individual portions, or into a larger ovenproof au gratin dish for family-style service, if you prefer.

19. Butter slices of stale bread on both sides, then cut into cubes. Put some of these on top of the ramekins or au gratin dish and broil. If you previously refrigerated this, then position the dish about 20cm (8 inches) from the heating element. If the contents are still warm because you just got it off the stove, then position the dish 15cm (6 inches) from the broiler. Cook until the bread cubes are golden. If they are slightly over-browned, it will still be fine. Keep a careful eye on the dish to avoid burning.

20. Finish with a little sprinkle of dried parsley flakes. The use of dried herbs as a finishing touch is one of those old school techniques that isn't commonly seen these days, but often works very well because the dried herb is more subdued in flavor and also cut extremely fine.

# SOME ADDITIONAL NOTES

The previous recipe was originally prepared slightly differently. The mushrooms were morels. The larger morels were halved and cooked in butter along with some minced shallots. Small morels were diced up and used the way the mushroom stems are here.

The Madeira called for in this recipe was originally a good French Sauternes, but this type of wine is considerably more expensive.

Finally, there were no buttered croutons on this dish originally. It was glazed under the broiler and then a few slices of black truffle were placed on top. On the topic of black truffles, beware that there are a lot of fake black truffles on the market since the discovery of an abundant fungus in China that looks almost exactly like a black truffle (although it has almost no flavor or aroma). Real black truffles are very expensive and very potent. The bogus type are completely worthless.

It is also worth mentioning that tastes have changed dramatically when it comes to wine and spirits in food. If you read books from long ago, the conventional wisdom was to always add the alcohol near the end of the cooking so that it would be strongly present. These days most people are not used to drinking as much liquor, so even a little bit in the food is often seen as objectionably "boozy" to the average diner. Therefore, I also modified the recipe to subdue the Madeira (originally Sauternes) by cooking most of it for longer so that the alcohol would have a chance to evaporate, just so you know. There are very few people these days who enjoy a dish that tastes like a cocktail, so that entire type of cuisine is practically extinct in restaurants today, but it was common decades ago.

# VENEZUELAN BLACKENED CHICKEN

*The classic Venezuelan version of this recipe is much simpler,*
*but as you get to the far north near Oaxaca, it is more complex.*

| | |
|---|---|
| 700g (1.5 lbs) | Chicken Thighs, bone-in |
| 2 t | Cumin Seeds |
| 1 1/4 t | Salt |
| 1 t | Dark Brown Sugar, preferably Cassonade |
| 1 t | Oregano, dried |
| 1 t | Turmeric (or 1 T freshly grated) |
| 1/2 t | Thyme, dried |
| 1/2 t | Smoked Paprika |
| 1 | Dried Green Chili Pepper (see note below) |
| 30ml (1 oz) | Lime Juice, fresh |
| 1/2 to 1 | Jalapeño Chili, minced (see note below) |
| 6 cloves | Garlic, crushed |
| 1 T | Ketchup |
| 1 t | Liquid Smoke |

## SEASONINGS

Ideally you want to use guajillo chilies for the dried one, but you can
substitute a dried green Serrano with good results. You can also make the
same substitution for the Jalapeño, if you have to.

Thyme is to chicken what cinnamon is to apples. We associate these
two flavors together strongly. Thyme isn't traditional, but it makes the
chicken stand out as chicken.

## ADDITIONAL TIPS

For a much milder flavor, substitute a teaspoon of Green Tabasco
Sauce for the fresh Jalapeño chili. I do this in Russia because Jalapeño
chilies are difficult to find and because most Russians don't like very
spicy food. This is already spicy because of the dried Serrano chili, too.

## PROCEDURE

1. Grind the cumin seeds, oregano, thyme, smoked paprika, dried chili pepper, salt, brown sugar, and also the turmeric if you are using dried (don't put freshly grated turmeric in your spice mill). Transfer to a bowl and mix with all of the other ingredients (except the chicken).

2. Slice two deep slashes into each leg and thigh. Spread the wet rub over both sides of the chicken and massage in. Let marinate at room temperature for 2 hours or refrigerate up to about 18 hours, but then allow an hour for the chicken to warm back up to room temperature before proceeding. Don't worry about it spoiling. The salt and acidity of the lime juice will protect it.

3. Spread the chicken out flat on a <u>metal</u> roasting pan, skin-side down. A thin (cheap) pan works best. Cook at 250°C (450°F) for 15-20 minutes. The first time you make this, experiment with a single piece of chicken to adjust the timing. You want it deeply caramelized on the skin-side, but not actually burnt.

4. Turn the pieces over. If the skin is already nicely blackened, then just put it back in the oven to roast for a few more minutes to ensure it is completely cooked. If the skin is still not dark enough, turn on your broiler and finish it up about 15cm (6 inches) from the heating element. This should take 5-10 minutes, depending on your broiler. In a restaurant, we intentionally stop short of it being blackened so that it can be finished up on demand when an order is placed (the final broiling also warms it up)..

4. Remove chicken to a platter and cool. This is especially well suited to serving with Cachapas (see the next recipe on page 82).

# CACHAPAS

*This is generally considered the national dish of Venezuela, yet somehow it is seldom seen in other parts of the world.*

| | |
|---|---|
| 200g (7 oz) | Corn, canned - drained |
| 15-20g (1/2 oz) | Cornmeal, fine (or regular all purpose flour) |
| 1 whole | Egg, extra-large |
| 1/2 t | Salt |
| 1 1/2 t | Bacon Fat, Duck Fat or Butter |
| 1/8 t | Onion Powder (optional) |
| Mozzarella Cheese, wet packed fresh | |
| Butter | |

## CORNMEAL

Cornmeal is sold in various different grinds ranging from almost as fine as flour to very coarse. You want finely ground cornmeal here. If you can't get it, then go ahead and use regular all-purpose white (wheat) flour. Coarse cornmeal is often sold for making grits or polenta. Don't use that kind because you will have a gritty result.

## ADDITIONAL TIPS

Commercial street vendors in Venezuela typically add light cream to this mixture so that it can be poured like pancake batter. This speeds production and lowers the cost, but it is actually not traditional. Grandmothers make it the way I'm showing here (without any cream added). If you want to make it the way the street vendors sell it, then thin it out with equal parts milk and cream (*i.e.* half and half). Everything else in the recipe is exactly the same. You will have some slightly burnt tasting skin formed, but it will fold easier and without breaking.

## PROCEDURE

1. In a food processor combine the corn, cornmeal, egg, salt, and the fat (or butter). Grind to the point where the corn is broken down to small pieces, but don't purée to a smooth liquid. Don't use a drink blender because it will grind everything too much. A food processor will take roughly a minute to combine it sufficiently, but it will still leave small pieces of corn, which is what you want.

2. Allow the mixture to rest for a minimum of 10 minutes, but an hour would be better. It isn't a problem if it sits for a couple of hours, either.

3. Melt 20-30 grams (3/4 to 1 oz) of butter with a little onion powder. You can use a microwave for this to make it easier.

4. Heat a nonstick pan (#6 out of 10) to about 160°C (320°F) and then brush with the melted butter / onion powder.

5. Ladle or spoon some of the mixture into the pan, smoothing it down with a spatula.

6. Cook until golden brown, then flip and finish cooking. See video for how this should look.

7. Place mozzarella cheese on half of the circle, then fold over. Brush with a little more of the melted butter / onion powder mixture. This goes especially well with the *Venezuelan Blackened Chicken* (see the previous recipe on page 80).

# SONORA MADELINES

*These savory madelines spiked with cumin are the perfect accompaniment to a Margarita before a Tex-Mex meal.*

| | |
|---|---|
| 150g (5.3 oz) | Flour |
| 100g (3.5 oz) | Butter, cut into smallish cubes |
| 30g (1 oz) | Dark Brown Sugar |
| 30g (1 oz) | Honey |
| 2 t | Cumin (see note below) |
| 2 whole | Eggs, large |
| 1 T | Onion, grated |
| 1 T | Lime Juice, fresh |
| 1 t | Lime Zest |
| 1/2 t | Baking Powder |
| 1/2 t | Baking Soda |
| 3/4 t | Salt |

## THE CUMIN

Ideally use cumin seeds that you grind yourself in a spice mill just prior to making this. Then don't grind them to a fine powder. Leave a little texture. This sort of "cracked cumin" is not available for purchase.

## ADDITIONAL TIPS

Use butter that has sat out of the refrigerator for about thirty minutes. You want it slightly soft, but not melted.

Be sure to actually grate the onion and not try to mince it with a knife. This will maximize the flavor of the onion without requiring much of it.

## PROCEDURE

1. Cream the butter with the dark brown sugar, ground cumin and salt.

2. To the mixer bowl (still with the paddle attachment), add the eggs and blend for about 30 seconds.

84

3. Add the grated onion, lime juice and lime zest. Run the mixer on a fairly slow speed while adding the flour, which you previously stirred the baking soda and baking powder into. Blend until it comes together, scraping down the sides, as necessary. Don't blend for more than about 2 minutes maximum.

4. Butter either madeline molds, or some other silicone form. You can use a silicone cupcake mold if that's all you have. Preheat oven to 200°C (390°F) with NO fan assist. Divide the mixture into the molds.

5.Baking time will depend on the shape and size of mold you are using. Anywhere from 10 to 20 minutes. The first time you make these you will have to judge them by sight and then adjust the time for the future, as is the nature of baking because there are many variables involved, including the airflow in your particular oven, the size of the mold you are using, the material of the mold, the altitude you are at, etc. Don't overcook them, though. They will still be edible, but lack the delicate flavor that compliments Margaritas so perfectly.

5. Let them cool on a wire rack for 15 minutes before unmolding. They can be eaten at that point, or stored, but be sure that they are at room temperature before putting them into a closed container or they will steam themselves into a soggy mess.

+

# ORECCHIETTE WITH MUSSELS

*This dish is bursting with flavor, which comes as a surprise to most people who cook it the first time because there seems to be surprisingly little in the way of seasoning if you measure by volume. Don't let the short ingredient list deceive you.*

| | |
|---|---|
| 90g (3 oz) | Mussels, shelled (see note below) |
| 90g (3 oz) | Orecchiette Pasta, ideally Casa Rinaldi |
| 35-40g (1.3 oz) | Butter |
| 30ml (1 oz) | White Wine, dry |
| 2 cloves | Garlic, cut in fine dice |
| 3/4 - 1 t | Seasoning Mixture (see note below) |
| 1/4 - 1/2 t | Chili Powder (see note below)) |
| Lemon (for juice) | |

## SEASONING MIXTURE AND CHILI POWDER

You can use the spice mixture in the video, but better results will be obtained with *LSD Seasoning Mix* (page 193).

The same thing goes for the chili powder. You can use a commercial product, but I strongly suggest using my blend (page 192).

## THE MUSSELS

You can use frozen mussels, but make sure that they are defrosted to close to room temperature before starting to cook this. Of course fresh mussels are even better, but don't choose ones that are huge.

## PROCEDURE

1. Start the pasta cooking in boiling salted water.

2. Melt the butter in a saucepan over a medium heat.

3. Add the garlic to the butter and cook <u>gently</u> for about 3 minutes.

4. Add the chili powder. Stir.

5. After about 2 minutes add the white wine and the seasoning mixture. Increase the heat to bring this to a boil for about 2 minutes

6. Lower the heat to a simmer. Cook to reduce until thickened some.

7. Add the mussels. Their relatively cold temperature will stop the mixture from simmering. Stir gently, maintaining the same lower heat until it comes to a simmer again.

8. Add the pasta (cooked to your personal preference of al dente, or otherwise). Stir to combine.

9. Increase heat slightly and continue stirring to drive off some of the moisture from the pasta.

10. Move the pan off the heat and put a lid on it. Allow it to stand for 2-3 minutes so the pasta can absorb some of the sauce.

11. Add about 2 teaspoons of lemon juice. Stir and then plate. You can garnish with a sprig of fresh herb, or roasted cherry tomatoes on the side, as you like.

DON'T BE THIS KIND OF COOK...

*I hate it when I'm hungry and go to the kitchen, and all there is are ingredients.*

# AFRICAN JOLLOF RICE

*There are many versions of this dish that dates back to the 14th century. The modern interpretation is usually made with chicken and curry powder, but this winds up tasting more like poorly made Indian food than the original classic dish.*

| | |
|---|---|
| 2 whole | Tomatoes, canned in juice |
| 150g (5.3 oz) | Onion, chopped |
| 2 cloves | Garlic, chopped |
| 1 1/2 t | Thyme, dried |
| 1/2 - 1 t | Nutmeg, ground (your preference) |
| 1 whole | Red Serrano Chili, dried |
| 1 whole | Red Serrano Chili, fresh (or Habañera) |
| 1/2 t | Dark Brown Sugar |
| 1 t | Ginger, grated |
| 1/4 t | Ground Black Pepper |
| 30ml (1 oz) | Palm Oil or vegetable oil |
| 120ml (7 oz) | Crayfish Stock or Shrimp Stock |
| 500ml (17.6 oz) | Beef Stock |
| 150g (2/3 cup) | Basmati Rice, rinsed under cold water |
| 150g (5.3 oz) | Ground Beef |
| 90g (3.2 oz) | Ham, cooked and cubed |
| 75g (2.6 oz) | Crawfish or Bay Shrimp, cooked |

## PROCEDURE

1. Heat a 4 liter (4 quart) pot on maximum heat (#10 out of 10) until very hot. Add enough oil to the bottom of the pan to coat it completely. Wait about 15 seconds for the oil to get hot, then add the 2 tomatoes. Use a splatter guard!

2. After the initial spitting has subsided a bit, lift the splatter guard (or lid) and break the tomatoes up a bit. Continue cooking on high heat. You want some actual blackening.

3. Add a little of the juice from the canned tomatoes. Cook until you just start to smell the first aroma of burning. Then reduce the heat to medium.

4. Add the onions to the pan. Use the moisture from the onions to help deglaze the pan by scraping the bottom. Cook 5 minutes with stirring.

5. Add the garlic, ginger and salt. Reduce heat to medium low (#3) and continue cooking with stirring for 5 more minutes.

6. Crumble the dried red chili in, but not the stem. Add the brown sugar.

7. After about 3 more minutes add the fresh red chili (diced). Stir for another couple of minutes.

8. Add the crawfish stock (or substitute, as explained earlier). Also add 1 teaspoon of the thyme (the rest will be used later) and the nutmeg now. Increase the heat back to medium (#5) and cook for about 2 minutes.

9. Increase the heat to maximum (#10). Add the ground meat and cook while stirring for 4-5 minutes.

10. When it is just short of burning, add a ladle of the beef stock. Then add the rice. Stir and continue cooking to nearly the point of burning. Add more stock to cool it off each time. See video for details.

11. When you have added about half of the stock, add the ham. Continue cooking and adding stock each time it gets close to burning.

12. When you have added about 3/4 of the stock, add the rest of the thyme and all the rest of the stock at once. Put a lid on it and reduce the heat to low (#2 out of 10).

13. Continue cooking for 10 minutes, but several times during this period lift the lid to stir the contents, scraping the bottom. - then return the lid.

14. Add the crawfish (or shrimp) and a little black pepper. Stir with the lid off until the seafood is warmed up. The rice should be completely cooked. Typically a bottled very hot habañero chili sauce is offered on the side.

# LAMB KORMA

*This is an unorthodox way of making this dish that was invented because we needed hundreds of portions and there was more oven space than stove top space available. Note that this is not the same as Chicken Korma, and in general you can not just swap meats out for each other in Indian curries and expect very good results.*

| | |
|---|---|
| 500g (17 1/2 oz) | Lamb Leg |
| 200g (7 oz) | Onion, sliced thin |
| 15g (1/2 oz) | Garlic cloves |
| 1 T | Ginger, grated |
| 1 or more | Green Serrano Chilies |
| 120g (4 oz) | Yogurt, plain (or half as much Greek yogurt) |
| 120g (4 oz) | Coconut Cream (see note below) |
| 1/4 cup | Cilantro (fresh), including stems |

## COCONUT CREAM

This is not the same as the sweetened canned coconut used in cocktails like a Pina Coladas. You can substitute part or all dairy cream, if you like.

| SPICE MIXTURE | |
|---|---|
| 2 1/2 t | Cumin Seeds |
| 3cm (1.2 inch) | Cinnamon stick |
| 1/2 t | Nutmeg, ground |
| 1/2 t | Black Peppercorns, whole |
| 1/2 t | Cloves, whole (the spice) |
| 1/4-1/2 t | Black Cumin Seeds (Nigella) |
| 2 whole | Brown Cardamom pods |
| 2 whole | Green Cardamom pods |
| 1 t | Coarse Salt |
| 22g (3/4 oz) | Smoked Almonds |

# PROCEDURE

1. Grind the salt and all of the spices listed above in an electric spice mill. Then grind the almonds. Combine the almonds with spices.

2. Remove the fat cap from the lamb. Discard it (or use for something else). Then cut away the meat from the bone. Save the bone for later use here. Cube up the meat, taking care to remove tendons and silver skin.

3. Massage the cubed lamb with the spices in a large bowl.

4. Lay the onions in an ovenproof rectangular tray (metal or ceramic). Put the bone on top and arrange the cubes of seasoned lamb around in a single layer on top of the onions. Roast at 200°C / 390°F for 45 minutes - 1 hour.

5. Strain the yogurt in a sieve, unless you are using Greek yogurt.

6. Soak the cilantro stems in water to loosen any dirt on them.

7. When the lamb comes out of the oven, remove the bone and meat to a bowl for later use. Put the cooked onions and all the juices into the cup of a stick blender. Add the garlic, green chilies, ginger, cilantro stems and the drained yogurt (the part that remained in the sieve, that is). Purée.

8. Put the bone in the center of a braising dish with a lid. Surround it with the cubes of lamb meat. Spread the puréed onion mixture over the top. Put the lid on and braise at 160°C / 320°F for 1 hour.

9. Remove the lid so you can stir the mixture, then return the lid and continue the braise at 120°C / 240°F for another 2 hours.

10. Discard the bone now. Add a little hot water to facilitate getting all of the contents of the braising dish out completely to a nonstick sauce pan. Add the coconut cream (or dairy cream) to the pan. Bring to a simmer.

11. Stir occasionally as it simmers for 45 minutes. Add water if it starts to get too dry, but don't add excess water—only enough to keep it the right consistency for a curry. Adjust salt and add red food coloring (if desired).

12. Partially cover and keep on a very low heat (#1) until perfectly tender. Add the rest of the cilantro and a little lemon juice in the last few minutes..

# CHILLI CON CARNE

*The milder venison version with red bell pepper is how it was being made at the Hotel Bel Air when I was there long ago.*

| | |
|---|---|
| 450g (16oz) | Beef or Venison |
| 150g (5oz) | Onion |
| 45g (1.5oz) | Bell Pepper or Chilies (see procedure below) |
| 30g (1 oz) | Bacon, fatty |
| 90ml (3oz) | Red Wine, dry (double this much for venison) |
| 6 cloves | Garlic, coarsely chopped |
| 3/4 t | Black Pepper, medium grind |
| 150g (5oz) | Tomato Purée (pasata) |
| 250ml (1 cup) | Beef Stock |
| | or substitute 1/2 Knorr beef gel pack & water |
| 2 t | Worcestershire Sauce |
| 30ml (1 oz) | Balsamic Vinegar |
| 180g (6.3oz) | Kidney Beans, canned |
| 1 T | Red Wine Vinegar (optional) |
| 2 1/2 - 3 T | Chlli Powder (page 192) |

## ADDITIONAL TIPS

Note that the chili powder is added a third at a time at different stages. Beans are optional. I suggest using them only with beef. In lieu of the red bell pepper, if you like your chilli extremely hot then substitute either a fresh red serrano chili pepper or (more extreme) habanero chilies. For the beef stock you can use 250ml of water and half of a *Knorr* Beef gel pack with good results. I suggest using beef shank for this because it has a lot of flavor and the long cooking time won't turn it into a paste.

## PROCEDURE

1. Cube up the meat. Add one tablespoon of the Chili Powder to the meat and mix well. Leave at room temperature for about an hour.

2. Dice the bacon and begin cooking in a 4 liter (4 quart) stock pot on a medium heat. Begin with the bacon in a cold pan.

3. After a few minutes when some fat has rendered from the bacon, add about half of the seasoned beef and increase heat to medium-high (#7).

4. When the pink has been cooked off of the surface of the meat, remove it to a platter and put the other half of the meat into the same pan to brown.

5. When the second half of the meat is browned, deglaze the pan with half of the red wine (leave that half of the meat in the pan during this).

6. When the pan is deglazed, transfer the meat to the same plater as the rest of the meat was placed. Now add the onion and bell pepper to the pan along with a little salt. Ideally use green bell pepper for beef and red bell pepper for venison. Substitute hot chilies for a very spicy version. Scrape the pan to get the rest of the fond up. Add any juices from the plottier of meat. Cook until the onion and peppers are caramelized - about 8 minutes. Don't burn them, though.

7. Add the garlic and reduce heat to medium-low (#4). After 2-3 minutes add the tomato purée. Scrape pan to pick up all of the remaining fond. Now add another tablespoon of the chili powder, stirring.

8. After another 2-3 minutes add the meat back to the pan. Increase heat to medium (#5) and add the ground black pepper.

9. After another 2-3 minutes add the rest of the wine. Cook one minute.

10. Add the beef stock, reduce heat to low (#3) and put a cover on. Simmer for 1 1/2 hours.

11. Add the Worcestershire sauce and cook another 30 minutes, covered.

12. Stir in the Balsamic vinegar, then cook another 60 minutes, covered.

13. Add another 1/2 to 1 tablespoon of Chili Powder and cook another 45 minutes. Add the beans during the last 15 minutes of cooking (optional).

# PASTA ALLA PUTTANESCA

*The concept of making a base sauce for dishes like this is a standard approach in fine dining restaurants, because it is physically impossible to produce deep flavors in a short amount of time. The base sauce is a bridge between the fresh ingredients and richness that only comes with the long cooking time that is physically necessary to produce deep flavors.*

### BASE SAUCE

| | |
|---|---|
| 300g (10.6 oz) | Puréed Tomatoes (pasata) |
| 45ml (1.5 oz) | Red Wine, dry |
| 45g (1.5 oz) | Onion, diced fine |
| 30g (1 oz) | Red Bell Pepper, diced fine |
| 4 cloves | Garlic, finely chopped |
| 1-2 | Anchovy, rinsed and chopped fine |
| | or 1 tablespoon of Thai Fish Sauce |
| 2 t | Dried Red Serrano Chili, crushed |
| | or substitute crushed red pepper flakes |
| Olive Oil | |

## PROCEDURE FOR THE BASE SAUCE

1. Heat a 4 liter (4 quart) sauce pan or stock pot (<u>not</u> nonstick) on a high heat (#8 out of 10) until it is very hot—about 200°C/400°F.

2. Add enough olive oil to coat the bottom surface of the pan in a complete layer. Wait about 30 seconds for it to get hot.

3. With a splatter guard standing by in one hand, add just over half of the puréed tomatoes to the pan with your other hand, then quickly cover with the screen. Do not stir! Resist the urge to stir this.

4. After the splattering has subsided, add the dried red chili and then return the splatter guard. Let it cook for about 4 minutes. Do not stir.

5. When the surface starts to look dry, add the diced bell pepper, onion and 3/4 teaspoon salt, scattering these across the top of the tomato sauce. Cook for another 2 minutes.

6. Add the rest of the tomato purée, and now you can finally stir it. Scrape the bottom to pick up the caramelized fond that formed.

7. Add the wine and the garlic and reduce heat to medium (#5). Stir occasionally, keeping it at a simmer for about 10 minutes.

8. Add the anchovy or Thai fish sauce. I prefer the latter. Cook another minute and then set aside. You can refrigerate this and store it so that you can prepare this recipe fairly quickly any time, since most of the time involved is in making this base sauce and it will keep for at least a week.

## THE PASTA

While this is traditionally served with spaghetti, it is more interesting with either cappelini or—going in the opposite direction—buccatini. Adjust the amount of the base sauce you use accordingly, with less for cappelini and more for buccatini.

| FOR THE PASTA | |
| --- | --- |
| 120g (4.2 oz) | Pasta, dried (see notes below) |
| 100g (3.5 oz) | Cherry Tomatoes, halved |
| * 30g (1 oz) | Chicken or Duck Liver, cooked (optional) |
| 16 | Black Olives, pitted |
| 1 1/2 T | Capers, rinsed (preferably salt packed) |
| 2 cloves | Garlic, sliced or whole (see video) |
| 2 | Anchovies, minced |
| Parmigiano Reggiano, Olive Oil, and Fresh Basil | |

## PROCEDURE FOR THE PASTA

1. Heat a pot of salted water to boiling and add the pasta.

2. Heat a nonstick skillet until it is about 100°C / 200°F (test with either an infrared thermometer or seeing drops of water boil off as shown in the video). Now add about 30ml (1 oz) of olive oil and wait 30 seconds.

3. Add the tomatoes and cook on a high heat (#8 out of 10) until some color develops. You want them to have surfaces that are actually starting to turn black. Don't completely burn them, of course.

4. Add the garlic, olives, capers and anchovy. Cook for about 2 minutes.

5. Add a portion of the base sauce you prepared. The exact amount will depend on what type of pasta you are using (less for thinner pasta) and your own personal preference. You can also add more crushed red pepper flakes, if you like it spicy. Stir and cook for 1-2 minutes.

6. Add the pasta to the pan. Stir and add some torn basil leaves. Cook for another minute or so. Plate with freshly grated parmesan topped with additional sprigs of fresh basil.

## OTHER INGREDIENTS

Duck liver is better than chicken liver for this if you can get it. Also, adding some duck meat and/or artichoke hearts—especially crisp deep fried artichoke hearts—lifts this dish up to the next level.

There has been some considerable controversy over whether to use black olives or green olives in this dish, mostly because one of the most respected authorities on Italian cuisine, Lidia Bastianich, publicly declared green olives as the "correct" choice. Historically there is no question that black olives were called for. Furthermore, in a taste test that I conducted in a restaurant with 48 guests sampling two versions of this dish, with the only difference being black vs. green olives, 46 reported they liked the black olives version more. Several identified the green olives specifically as the problem.

# THE PUTANESCA LEGEND

Italy is rich in fables about how various dishes got their name, especially pastas. One of the most famous legends is that of Putanesca, because the word means prostitute (but it also has another meaning). This was undoubtedly the inspiration for the story that tells of prostitutes making this dish so the aroma would lure hungry men inside the brothel. The first problem with this story is that brothels were outlawed in Italy in 1958 and Putanesca wasn't invented until the 1960's.

The word putanesca has another meaning which doesn't translate into English very well. It literally means garbage, but rather in the sense of too many ingredients in a dish. Remember that traditional Italian cuisine is about simplicity—a few high quality ingredients prepared in a simple way.

*A vintage Italian street sign advertising the prices of various services available at the brothel located inside. Circa 1930's.*

# SALMON CURRY

*Salmon has only recently been available in India, so there are no traditional recipes for it. This is based on a Goan fish curry with some changes made to optimize it for salmon. Notice how the curry ingredients are divided. The coriander goes on the fish, but the cumin seeds cook with the sauce.*

SPICE BLEND

| | |
|---|---|
| 1 t | Coriander Seeds, whole |
| 2.5cm (1") piece | Cinnamon Stick |
| 1 whole | Dried Red Serrano Chili |
| 1/2 t | Mustard Seeds, preferably brown |
| 4 | Cloves, whole (the spice) |
| 4 | Green Cardamom pods |
| 4 | Allspice, whole |
| 1 1/2 t | Dark Brown Sugar, ideally Cassonade |
| 1 t | Salt |
| 1/4 t | Citric Acid |

## WILD VS. FARMED SALMON

Both wild and farmed salmon are low in mercury and other established harmful pollutants. Farmed salmon has a much higher fat content, but is also much higher in Omega-3 oils, which are beneficial to health. Farmed salmon is more forgiving of overcooking and it costs much less. For these reasons farmed salmon is

## PROCEDURE

1. Toast the coriander seeds, cinnamon stick, dried chili, mustard seeds, cloves, cardamom and allspice until the mustard seeds start to pop. This stage is especially important to do right in this recipe, so consult the video for specific instructions.

2. After allowing the toasted spices to cool for a few minutes, put them into an electric spice grinder along with the dark brown sugar, salt and citric acid. Grind to a powder. This spice is used in two places ahead...

| | |
|---|---|
| 300g (10.5 oz) | Salmon fillet |
| 45g (1.5 oz) | Onion, chopped |
| 1 T | Garlic, crushed |
| 1 t | Cumin Seeds, whole |
| 1 whole | Bay Leaf |
| 1-2 T | Ginger, peeled and cut into strips |
| 1 whole | Green Serrano Chili, fresh |
| 90g (3 oz) | Tomato Purée (pasata) |
| 110g (4 oz) | Coconut Cream (not sweetened) |
| | or substitute dairy cream, or a mix of the two |

For presentataion: butter, lemon juice, fresh cilantro

3, In a small bowl combine a tablespoon of the spice mixture you just prepared with the tablespoon of crushed garlic and a tablespoon of oil or ghee. Stir to combine and add red food coloring, if desired.

4. Coat the salmon with this marinade. Refrigerate for 1 to 4 hours.

5. Begin by frying the onions in 1-2 tablespoons of oil or ghee on a medium heat (#6 out of 10). Cook until translucent.

6. Add the cumin seeds, green chili pepper and ginger. Cook for about 3 more minutes while stirring.

7. Add 2 teaspoons of the spice mixture and the bay leaf. After 30 seconds add the tomato purée. Continue cooking with stirring. Lower heat a bit.

8. After about 10 minutes it will get very thick. Now turn the heat down further (#3) and place the salmon filet on top of the masala. Cover and cook for about 6 minutes, then turn the piece over, cover again, and continue cooking for another 3 minutes. Note that the time will be longer if your salmon is very thick, or less if your salmon is very thin. Remember that the salmon will be cooked a little more at the end under the broiler, so don't worry if it is a bit too rare right now.

9. Carefully remove the salmon to a plate with a wide spatula to keep from breaking the fish into pieces. Gently scrape off any chunks of spice or onions that are clinging to the salmon, being careful not to damage the surface.

10. Add the coconut cream (or dairy cream) to the pan that you removed the salmon from. Whisk while heating on medium (#5 out of 10). Bring to a simmer, but don't boil it. Cook for 2-3 minutes.

11. Pass the sauce through a sieve. Rub to get as much through as possible. At this point you can refrigerate the sauce and the fish and finish it off on demand, or simply hold it here until guests arrive, if needed.

12. If you have refrigerated the fish first, then you need to preheat your oven to 190°C / 375°F before switching to the broiler so that the fish will warm back up in the middle at the same time the outside is being browned. Adjust the rack in your oven so that the salmon is about 20cm (8 inches) from the broiler heating element. Cook until golden on top. The time will depend on the strength of your broiler, which vary greatly from stove to stove.

13. Brush on some melted butter and sprinkle with a little lemon juice. Spoon reheated sauce onto a plate and place the fish on the sauce. Garnish with freshly picked cilantro leaves.

# MORE NOTES ON FISH

When I wrote that salmon has only recently became available in India, I am referring to the type of salmon that is primarily caught in Alaska and Norway. There is a very popular fish in India known as "rawas" that is often called Indian Salmon. However, the flesh is white and the taste is quite different. It is much lower in Omega-3 oils, too. It is a good tasting fish, but it is not what people in other parts of the world call salmon.

One should be aware that in many parts of the world, especially the United States, many species of fish are all lumped together and sold under a single name. This is partly to eliminate confusion from consumers, and partly a business decision so that markets can maintain an inventory of each important category of fish at the most affordable price at the time.

This is much less the case in regions of the world where fish is a vital component in the diet. In Goa, for instance, there are more than 130 different local fish sold by individual names. When you buy one, you are getting that specific fish and not just something similar. Contrast this with UK and American fish markets, where between 25% and 93% of the fish sold as "cod" is actually some other inferior species. Some high end American markets have taken to actually stating "true cod" on displays because the expectation of fraud among wary consumers is so high.

Finally, beware of farmed fish from southeast Asia. These are often raised in highly polluted waters and are unsafe to consume. Some countries have banned the import, but there are ways around this for exporters. For example, Vietnamese catfish is banned from importation to the United States, but the ban does not extend to two other similar species that are brought in and sold as "catfish" in American discount stores. Be especially careful about shrimp, too. The best thing you can do is find an actual fishmonger and consult with them. As is often the case in life, you get what you pay for.

# THAI DUCK & PINEAPPLE CURRY

*This is really an American version of Thai food rather than an authentic dish, but it is delicious never the less.*

| | |
|---|---|
| 150g (5.3 oz) | Duck Meat, cooked (see note below) |
| 160g (5.6 oz) | Onion, cored and coarsely chopped |
| 150g (5.3 oz) | Pineapple, canned is okay (fresh is better) |
| 45g (1.5 oz) | Red Bell Pepper, cut into strips |
| 30g (1 oz) | Cashew Nuts |
| 2-3 whole | Green Serrano Chilies, diced |
| 22g (3/4 oz) | Garlic, chopped |
| 15g (1/2 oz) | Ginger, grated |
| 1 stalk | Lemongrass |
| 22g (3/4 oz) | Peanut Oil, or substitute vegetable oil |
| 1 t | Nam Pla (Thai fish sauce) |
| 1/2 - 1 t | Red Pepper Flakes |
| Cilantro (fresh), Lime (for juice) | |

## COOKED DUCK

I use duck confit in this recipe because it works fine and duck legs are much less expensive than duck breasts. After the confit process, the meat is quite resistant to becoming dry or tough, which is a great advantage. In the video I include how to prepare the duck confit, but here I am treating the cooked duck as an ingredient that you should have already prepared.

| | FOR THE SAUCE |
|---|---|
| 400g (14.1 oz) | Light Duck Stock |
| 150ml (5.3 oz) | Pineapple Juice |
| 90g (3.2 oz) | Sugar |
| 60ml (2 oz) | Apple Cider Vinegar |
| small piece | Ginger |
| 1 T | Soy Sauce |
| 1/2 t | MSG (optional) |

## PROCEDURE

1. Combine all of the ingredients for the sauce (see list above) except the soy sauce in a 2 liter (2 quart) sauce pan and bring to a simmer.

2. Keep at a slow simmer until it is reduced to the point of thickening, as shown in the video.

3. Remove from the heat, stir in the soy sauce and set aside. You can do this days in advance and store it in the refrigerator.

4. Bash the lemongrass with the back of a heavy knife.

5. Heat a large stockpot or wok on a medium high heat (#7 out of 10).

6. When it is hot, add the peanut oil. Wait a few seconds for the oil to get hot, then add the onion and the lemongrass. Cook for about 5 minutes.

7. Add the garlic, ginger, green chilies and red pepper flakes. Cook with stirring for about 3 minutes.

8. Add the cashews. Stir frequently to keep the garlic from burning.

9. After another minute add the red bell pepper. Continue stirring.

10. After another couple of minutes add the duck meat and the pineapple. Continue stirring for another 1-2 minutes. Lower heat slightly (#6).

11. Add a little lime juice and the previously made sauce you reduced. Scrape the bottom of the pan to deglaze it. Cook for another minute.

12. Add the Thai fish sauce (nam pla) and cilantro.

13. Taste and adjust the salt level. Consider adding a dash of sugar if needed. Remove from the heat and cover. Let it stand for 1-2 minutes.

14. Take the lemongrass out before plating. Add a little more lime juice and sprigs of fresh cilantro.

# ROASTED PORK
# (KOREAN STYLE)

*This version is a bit different from the video. The results of this have many applications. An example is on the next page.*

| | |
|---|---|
| 500g (17.6 oz) | Pork, not too lean (shoulder or neck) |
| 1 whole | Kiwi fruit, peeled |
| 1 whole | Shallot, peeled |
| 2 T | Vegetable Oil |
| 2 t | MSG (or 1 t salt, if you prefer) |
| 1/2 t | Black Pepper, ground |

## KIWI FOR TENDERIZING

Kiwi fruit is rich in the protease enzyme, *actinidin*. It is very popular in Korea as a meat tenderizer. The academic journal, *Food Chemistry* (1 September 2012, Pages 95–105), shows that actinidin is the most effective enzyme at breaking down meat proteins. The enzymes *papayan* (from papaya) and *bromelein* (from pineapple) are considerably less effective.

## ADDITIONAL TIPS

I suggest using a Jaccard device on the pork before you cube it and marinate it. This will allow the marinade to penetrate deeper, too.

## PROCEDURE

1. Purée the peeled kiwi with the shallot, oil, MSG and black pepper.

2. Cut the pork into large cubes. Mix it well with the kiwi marinade. Stir once in a while over the span of 30-40 minutes.

3. During this time preheat your oven to 180°C / 360°F. Arrange a wire rack over a baking sheet or pan. Place the pork on the wire rack.

4. Turn the oven to broil and position the pork on the wire rack about 15cm (6 inches) from the heating element. Cook for about 15 minutes to brown it well.

5. Turn the pieces over and broil on the other side for about 3 minutes. Remove and allow to cool. The meat is now ready for many different sauces and applications, and should be both tender and flavorful.

# ROASTED PORK WITH MUSHROOMS

*Here is a simple example of how this pork can be used. Remember you can refrigerate the cooked pork to use later, too.*

## PROCEDURE

1. Use about the same volume of mushrooms as you have of cooked pork from the previous recipe here. Porcini mushrooms are ideal for this. If the mushrooms are large, slice them. In a large pan, brown the mushrooms in vegetable oil, working in batches so as not to overcrowd the pan.

2. Set the mushrooms aside and add about half the weight of chicken broth plus several cloves of garlic (peeled and chopped). You can use water and a Knorr chicken gel pack, if you need to. Keep at a good simmer and deglaze the pan from the mushroom residue.

3. Continue cooking the garlic in the chicken broth until reduced in volume by about half. Now add the mushrooms and the cooked pork back to the pan. Stir to combine and cook about 5 minutes uncovered.

4. Add 2 tablespoons of the *1890's Meat Sauce* (page 108), or regular ketchup if you don't have that available. Stir to combine. Taste and adjust salt. Set the stove heat to very low (#1 out of 10) and put a lid on it.

5. Cook for about 30 minutes, stirring once or twice during this time.

6. Remove from the heat and allow to cool with the lid on for another few minutes before serving.

# BEEF CHEEKS WITH MUSHROOMS

*Loosely based on a dish showcased on one of the Australian MasterChef episodes by a Michelin star chef. I have modified it to make it more accessible and less expensive.*

| | COATING FOR THE BEEF |
|---|---|
| 15g (1/2 oz) | Dried Tomatoes (see note below) |
| 1 t | Rosemary, dried |
| 1 t | Basil, dried |
| 1 t | Salt |
| 3/4 t | Black Peppercorns |
| 1 T | Balsamic Vinegar |
| 1 T | Olive Oil |

## DRIED TOMATOES

The dried tomatoes called for in this recipe are completely dried to the point of being solid enough that they can be ground to a powder. These can often be purchased, but you may have to look online. You can prepare your own in the same way that you dry chilies in the oven overnight, but I advise you to put the tomato slices on either a silicone mat or some good quality parchment paper to minimize sticking. For more about dried tomatoes, see page 23.

| | |
|---|---|
| 500g (18 oz) | Beef, ideally Beef Cheek |
| 10g (1/3 oz) | Dried Porcini Mushrooms |
| 8 whole | Large Mushrooms, separated into stems & caps |
| 60g (2 oz) | Shallots |
| 60g (2 oz) | Demi-glace |
| 1 whole | Bay Leaf |
| Fresh Basil leaves for garnish | |

## PROCEDURE

1. Grind together the dried tomatoes with the herbs, salt and peppercorns.

2. Coat the beef with the dry mixture as evenly as possible. Now add the balsamic vinegar and olive oil and massage the meat together. Refrigerate for at least 3 hours and preferably overnight.

3. Roast the dried porcini mushrooms in a pan at 160°C / 320°F for 15 minutes. Cool to room temperature and then grind to a powder in an electric spice mill. This can be done up to two weeks in advance.

4. Heat a pan and add enough olive oil to coat the bottom of a heavy nonstick pan. A quality pan will make a big difference in the result - very heavy and in good shape. Fry the cubes of beef in the pan on a medium-high heat (#7 out of 10) to brown them, working in batches. Don't burn the coating on the meat. Refer to the video.

5. Add 250ml (1 cup) of water to the bowl that the beef had been marinading in to pick up any leftover marinade and juices. When the beef has finished browning, add the shallots and mushroom stems (only the stems at this point) and deglaze the pan with the water/leftover marinade..

6. After 3-4 minutes, transfer the contents to a pressure cooker. Add the rest of the water/leftover marinade, the browned beef and the demi-glace. Cook at pressure for 45-50 minutes.

7. Transfer the shallots, beef stock and the meat to a pressure cooker. cook for 45-50 minutes so that only wisps of steam are escaping.

8. Remove the meat and set aside. Strain off the juices from the pressure cooker into a fat separating pitcher. Discard solids from the strainer and the liquid fat that floats to the top. Add the bay leaf to the broth and reduce until thick. Now add the meat back into the thickened liquid to reheat it.

9. Thinly slice the mushroom caps and dust with the roasted porcini powder. Arrange on plates with a few fresh basil leaves, as shown in the video.

# 1890's MEAT SAUCE

*Aside from being used directly on meats, you can use this as a substitute for ketchup in salad dressings or any other recipe calling for ketchup. The advantage being that it will have far more complexity and sophistication. This works especially well on hamburgers and hot dogs, and I would never use regular ketchup on the latter.*

| | |
|---|---|
| 120g (4.2 oz) | Tomato Purée (pasata) |
| 40g (1.4 oz) | Raisins, golden |
| 40ml (1.4 oz) | Cider Vinegar |
| 2 T | Dried Beet Powder (see below) |
| 1 small | Anchovy, rinsed in two changes of water |
| 1 T | Dark Brown Sugar |
| 2 t | Sugar (white) |
| 1 t | Malt Vinegar or Sherry Vinegar |
| 1 t | Salt |
| 1/2 t | Marjoram, dried |
| 1/4 t | Cayenne Pepper |
| 1/8 t | Black Pepper, finely ground |
| 15g (1/2 oz) | Onion, raw |

## DRIED BEET POWDER

When I was a child I liked reading the labels on bottled sauces because the ingredients were often quite surprising.. This was before the FDA allowed manufacturers to conceal their recipe with vague terms like "natural flavorings". Everything was spelled out. One popular brand of sauce listed dried beet powder as an ingredient and I found this especially amusing. I tried to imagine the day in development when someone at the factory tasted it and boldly declared that what it was lacking was dried beets! The idea seemed laughably implausible, so how did it ever come about? I thought about this from time to time for many years. Eventually I came to realize that I was looking at the problem through the wrong end of the telescope. Beets are inexpensive. Dry roasting them is not an expensive process. So here is an inexpensive product with a unique taste that food technicians could go to work with to invent an original product. Dress it up with some sugar, salt and other cheap ingredients and you have a unique sauce that is inexpensive to produce and can't be easily duplicated. Especially once you stop telling people what's in it by changing the label to read only, "natural ingredients". The thing is that dried beets really do bring a novel flavor to a sauce that is especially well suited to meats. This is my own recipe that takes advantage of dried beets as a flavoring.

For directions on drying the beets and more about this topic, see the table of contents under *Dried Vegetables*. As I explain in that section, the dry roasted powder tastes very different from the fresh vegetable, so even if you hate beets, I promise you that this won't taste like beets.

## PROCEDURE

1. Allow the raisins to sit in the cider vinegar for at least several hours, covered. Overnight or even 24 hours is better still.

2. Combine all of the ingredients in in a small saucepan and bring to a simmer on a medium-low heat (#4 out of 10). Cook for 20 minutes, stirring occasionally.

3. Transfer the contents of the pan to the cup of a stick blender. Add the raw onion to the cup and purée.

4. Rub through a fine sieve. Discard solids, or use in a soup.

5. Store in a small jar in the refrigerator. It needs to rest for at least one day for the flavors to meld. This keeps for a long time in the refrigerator.

# SMOKED CLAM CHOWDER WITH CELERY ROOT AND SCOTCH WHISKY

*This is technically a type of New England Clam Chowder, but it really belongs in a category by itself because it has several ingredients that are not traditional and celery root is used in place of potatoes. In Russia soup is a vital part of any good restaurant's menu. It is expected to be made from scratch and a measure of the restaurant's status. This soup received unanimous praise in several Russian restaurant reviews, with one writer saying it was the best soup of his entire life.*

| | |
|---|---|
| 100g (3.5 oz) | Smoked Clams, canned |
| 300g (10.6 oz) | Celery Root (celeriac) |
| 400ml (14.1 oz) | Milk (or part cream) |
| 30g (1 oz) | Shallot |
| 1/2 t | Ajwain (see note below) |
| 3/4 t | White Pepper, ground |
| 30g (1 oz) | Butter |
| 2 T | Flour |
| 1 | Bay Leaf |
| 1 T | Lemon Juice |
| dash | Scotch Whisky |
| 1-2 | Scallions, sliced very thin (as a garnish) |

## AJWAIN

This is a spice that is similar to the herb thyme. You can substitute thyme if you can't get ajwain, but the results will not be quite as good.

## ADDITIONAL TIPS

If the soup is too thick then feel free to thin it to the desired consistency with water, milk or even cream. Obviously adding more cream will make it extremely rich, which is perfectly fine if you are serving a tiny portion of this as a starter course in a large meal. If it is a meal by itself, then cream will make it too heavy for many people.

## PROCEDURE

1. Deep peel the celery root. Discard the peel. Now make slices. Trim the round edges from each slice to make squares. The rounded edges you trimmed off will also be used. Now that you have square slices, you can cut them into even sized dice.

2. Add the trimmed curved edges of the slices to a pot of salted water and bring to a boil. Keep at a good simmer about 30 minutes until very soft.

3. Lift the pieces out with a spider or slotted spoon and set aside for later use. Into the same water you just boiled the edge pieces, add the nicely cut cubes of celery root and return to a rapid simmer for 10-15 minutes.

4. In another nonstick sauce pan, make a roux with the flour and butter. Cook with stirring over a medium (#4 out of 10) heat until it is just past blonde. Do not turn up the heat to try and rush making a roux—ever.

5. Whisk in the milk to make a simple Bechamel.

6. Put about half of the Bechamel you just made in the cup of a stick blender with the boiled celery root <u>edge pieces</u> and the shallots. Purée.

7. Pour the purée back into the pan with the rest of the Bechamel. Add the bay leaf and the evenly cut cubed pieces of celery root. Also add the smoked clams along with the juices from the can. Heat gently. Do not boil.

8. Bring it to a very gentle simmer. Add the ground white pepper and freshly ground ajwain (use a mortar and pestle). Stir. Taste and adjust the salt level. This will vary widely depending on how salty your clams were.

9. Keep at a simmer for 6-8 minutes and no longer. Remove the bay leaf and stir in the lemon juice and the Scotch Whisky. Plate up, garnishing with a few thinly sliced scallions.

# DUCK WITH WHITE BEANS, DRIED PLUMS AND FRIED SAGE

*We are so accustomed to pairing duck with sweet fruit that we easily forget that it also has a rich savory taste, too. Although the seasoning on this is primarily made from dry roasted plums, the result is very rich and packed with umami goodness.*

| | |
|---|---|
| 2 | Duck breasts |
| 250g | White Beans, canned (rinsed and drained) |
| 1 | Shallot, diced |
| 1 clove | Garlic, sliced |
| 3 t | Dried Plum Spice Mix (page 200) |
| 2 T | Scallions, chopped |
| few leaves | Sage, fresh (for garnish) |

## DUCK BREASTS

Select large duck breasts for this. Normally these are more difficult to cook, but in this case because they are cooked a second time, this will help make sure that the duck remains tender.

## PROCEDURE

1. Rub skin-side of duck breasts with coarse salt. Place skin-side down on a nonstick skillet that's been heated to about 100°C / 200°F (to test, water droplets just start to boil). Set the heat to medium (#5 to 6 out of 10).

2. Sprinkle the up-side of each duck breast with half a teaspoon of the Dried Plum Spice Mix (the rest will be used later).

3. When a lot of fat accumulates in the pan, drain it off. Don't drain it every few seconds, though! Reserve the fat for later. Cook about 90% of

the way to rare on the skin-side down. Then flip them over for a little more cooking, moving around the pan (see video).

4. Transfer to a plate and rest until they come to room temperature.

5. Cut the skin off of each piece. Slice into strips. Heat a nonstick skillet with enough water to cover the bottom of the pan. Put the duck skin into the pan (immersed in the water) skin-side down. Heat pan to medium and let it cook until the water has evaporated, the fat renders.

6. After 20-30 minutes the pieces will have curled up. Now flip them over and put a weight on top of them, such as a pan partly filled with water. Turn the heat off completely and let it sit for 10-15 minutes.

7. While you are waiting for this, heat a small pot of oil to about 185°C / 365°F and deep fry the sage leaves briefly (about 10 seconds). Set aside.

8. Drain the duck skin on paper towel and apply salt. Set aside for later.

9. Cube up the duck breasts. Toss in a bowl with the other 2 teaspoons of the Dried Plum Spice Mix. Set aside.

10. Heat a large sauce pan or small stock pot on a medium-low heat (#4). Add the reserved duck fat, the shallots and the garlic. Sweat 4-5 minutes.

11. Add the white beans and increase the heat to medium-high (#7 1/2 out of 10). Cook until there is some visible color on the beans and your start to hear some popping. Don't stir them too much, or they will break up.

12. Add the cubed duck breast and the scallions. Turn the heat off and let the residual heat do the cooking. Stir to combine and then cover and let stand for about 3 minutes.

13. Taste and adjust the seasoning. As I wrote in the annotations at the end of this video, always taste the food and don't feel shy to add salt, pepper, lemon juice, olive oil, a pinch of cayenne, a dash of MSG, or anything else that it might need to punch it up. Maximizing flavor while maintaining balance are your unwavering goals. Plate this up with the fried sage and pieces of the crisp duck skin.

✦

# DOPPLEBOCK BEEF

*This is generally used as an ingredient in other more complex dishes, as explained in the video.*

| | |
|---|---|
| 700g (25 oz) | Beef, Top Sirloin or Short Loin |
| 2 t | Bittersweet Paprika (see page 23) |
| 90g (3 oz) | Onion, sliced |
| 4-5 cloves | Garlic, cut in halves |
| 160ml (5.5 oz) | Dopplebock Beer (see below) |
| 2 T | Olive Oil |
| 2 T | Smetana, 30% fat, or Crème Fraîche |
| 1 branch | Rosemary, fresh |
| Coarse Salt, Black Pepper | |

## DOPPLEBOCK BEER

Spaten's *Optimator* is a good choice. *Salvator* from Paulaner is another excellent choice. Although not dopplebocks, you can also obtain good results with Spaten *Dunkel* (Germany) and one of my personal favorites for this recipe, Belhaven *90/- Wee Heavy* (Scotland). The key is that you want strong malt and very low bitterness. I strongly advise against using either Sam Adams *Double Bock*, Eku *28*, or pretty much any other ale with more than 9% alcohol. It isn't the alcohol that's the problem, but the process that led up to that high alcohol concentration.

## ADDITIONAL TIPS

Smetana is a type of sour cream, only not nearly as sour and with more fat. It is rarely seen in the United States, just as American sour cream is almost nonexistent in Russia. Here it helps control the bitterness and keeps the meat from drying out. Sour cream is not a good substitute, but crème fraîche is.

*114*

# PROCEDURE

1. Cut the meat into large pieces, removing any thick bands of connective tissue that won't break down. Season with coarse salt.

2. In a large nonstick pan (you can use your pressure cooker for this if it is nonstick), brown the meat well in the olive oil over fairly high heat (#8 out of 10), working in two or three batches. Add more olive oil it starts to get dry so it might burn. Develop a good crust.

3. Reduce heat to medium (#5 out of 10) and add the sliced onions and deglaze the pan with all of the beer at once. Scrape the bottom of the pan.

4. Transfer to the pressure cooker, if you were doing the first stage in a separate nonstick pan. Sprinkle the meat with the paprika. After about 3 minutes add the garlic, then the meat with any juices and extra paprika that didn't stick. Also add the smetana (or crème fraîche) and put the branch of rosemary in. You can also add a branch of fresh thyme if you have it. Put the lid on the pressure cooker.

5. As soon as it comes to pressure, as evidenced by wisps of steam escaping from the valve, reduce the heat to very low to keep it just below the point where excess pressure escapes. Cook for 1 1/2 hours.

6. Remove from the heat, but leave it sealed for another 30 minutes. This lets the liquid re-absorb into the meat.

7. Now open it up and transfer the pieces of meat to a container. Discard the branches of herbs and pass the liquid through a fine mesh sieve.

8. Cover the liquid and refrigerate overnight. The next day you can peel the solidified fat off (it is used in the *Dopplebock Beef Potatoes* recipe on page 116).

You can store the beef and the de-fatted broth in the freezer for up to several months and use it for many other recipes. One example is the *Azerbaijan Plov* (page 68).

# POTATOES FROM DOPPLEBOCK BEEF

*This is what is classified as a "beer snack" in Russia, being something salty, savory and sometimes a bit spicy, usually being a bread or potato dish. It also makes a good side dish.*

| | |
|---|---|
| 200g (7 oz) | Potatoes - waxy variety (not starchy) |
| 2 T | Dopplebock Beef Fat (see below) |
| 120g (4 oz) | Onion (optional) |
| 1 T | Butter |
| Black Pepper, fresh ground | |

## DOPPLEBOCK BEEF FAT

This is a byproduct from making the Dopplebock Beef recipe (see previous two pages). You can substitute rendered bacon fat or duck fat with good results, but obviously they won't have the same seasoning that the Dopplebock Beef fat provides.

## ADDITIONAL TIPS

The onion in the water you cook the potatoes in adds a subtle background flavor that is beneficial in many recipes calling for boiled potatoes, such as gnocchi. I save the root end of cut onions for this application because they would be trash otherwise and the root holds it together during the boiling time.

## PROCEDURE

1. Peel and then cut the potatoes into roughly equal size pieces just over 1 centimeter (a half inch) on each side.

2. Put the onion in a pot of water on the stove (if you are using it) and bring to a rapid boil.

3. Add the potatoes to the boiling water. The exact amount of time will depend on what specific type of potato you are using. About 6 minutes should be right, but make a note here in the book to record the type of potato you used and whether the time should have been a bit more or less based on the outcome. Here's a space for writing:

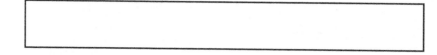

4. Drain the potatoes in a colander and allow them to cool to room temperature before proceeding.

5. Transfer the potatoes to a mixing bowl and pour the Dopplebock Beef Fat over them. Mix gently to avoid breaking up the potatoes. Preheat oven to 200°C / 400°F.

6. Sprinkle with fresh ground black pepper. Spread them out in a single layer on a nonstick pan that can be used both on top of the stove and in the oven. Many good quality pans have detachable handles to allow them to go into the oven. You can use a thinner pan such as a cookie sheet or a cake pan, but you risk burning the pieces. Roast for 20 minutes.

7. Remove from the oven, shake to make sure nothing is sticking. Sprinkle with salt and return to the oven for another 20 minutes.

8. Now remove from the oven and either re-attach the handle, or transfer to a mixing bowl and add the butter. Toss to melt the butter and coat the pieces. Now put them back into the oven again (if you tossed them with the butter in a bowl, transfer them back to the cookie sheet or cake pan). Cook for the final 15-20 minutes.

9. Mix with freshly minced herbs. Dill works well. Scallions are also very good, or you can omit the herbs entirely if you prefer.

# CARROT AND WHITE CHOCOLATE RISOTTO

*No, this is not a dessert, and as you probably guessed, it is not a classic Italian dish, either.*

| | |
|---|---|
| 150g (5.3 oz) | Carnaroli Rice, or Arborio (not as good) |
| 800ml (28 oz) | Stock, ideally Duck (see notes below) |
| 60g (2 oz) | Carrot, finely grated |
| 45ml (1.5 oz) | Cognac or Brandy |
| 30g (1 oz) | Butter, cut in pieces and put in the freezer |
| 30g (1 oz) | Shallots, diced fine |
| 30g (1 oz) | Parmesan Cheese, grated |
| 30g (1 oz) | White Chocolate (see notes below) |
| 1-2 T | Olive Oil, extra-virgin |
| 1 t | Sherry Vinegar (optional) |
| 1/4 t | Bittersweet Paprika (optional) |
| Sage, dried (for more about this, see page 21) | |

## WHITE CHOCOLATE

There are many types of white chocolate and the type you choose will determine the outcome of this dish. Unfortunately, most products sold as "white chocolate" are mostly sugar flavored with vanilla. For the best results I recommend E. Guittard's 31% Cacao Pure White Chocolate Wafers. You will probably have to resort to online shopping for this product. Crumble the white chocolate to small pieces before adding it.

## ADDITIONAL TIPS

While a good duck stock will take take this to the realm of a Michelin star restaurant, the results are still vert good with chicken stock. If you want to push it over the fence toward being more savory, add the bittersweet paprika (see page 23). I don't suggest using regular paprika.

## PROCEDURE

1. Sweat the shallots in a little olive oil for 4-5 minutes on a medium-low heat.

2. Add the rice to the pan and increase the heat to medium. Stir the rice and toast it until there is a nutty aroma. About 3-4 minutes.

3. Add the cognac. Stir and evaporate off the liquid in the same way you would with white wine in a traditional risotto. If you are going to add the bittersweet paprika, now is the time to do so.

4. When it is nearly dry, add the first ladle of stock and increase the heat to medium-high (about 7 1/2 out of 10). Begin counting the time. The key to consistent results is watching the clock. Your active participation will be needed for the next 17 minutes straight.

5. Stir frequently. Each time it reaches near-dryness, add another ladle of stock. Continue doing this until 12 minutes have elapsed.

6. Add the finely grated carrots. Continue stirring, and add another ladle of stock if needed. Continue for about 2 minutes.

7. Add the white chocolate and stir. Add more stock as needed.

8. After another 2 minutes (16 minutes now since the first ladle of stock was added), mix in the Parmesan cheese and a little of the crumbled dried sage. Also add the last of the stock. It should be fairly liquidy now, but it will tighten up some as it finishes cooking.

9. When another minute has passed (17 minutes now since the first ladle of stock was added), beat in the frozen pieces of butter vigorously until it has all melted.

10. Remove the pan from the heat, cover and rest for 4-5 minutes. Taste it and adjust the salt level. If it is a bit too sweet, add the sherry vinegar. You may also want to add a teaspoon or two more cognac.

# BLUE CHEESE STUFFED STEAK

*This is one of those ideas that looks great on paper, but is very difficult to execute well. Two problems plague you. First, blue cheese has a low melting point, so it will run out as a liquid before the meat is cooked. Second, the potency of the blue cheese can easily overpower the steak so that all you taste is spongy, bloody roquefort. This approach solves both problems to yield exactly what everyone hopes for in this superb pairing.*

| | |
|---|---|
| 2 | Ribeye Steaks, 3cm (1.25") thick |
| 30g (1 oz) | Shallots, chopped finely |
| 30g (1 oz) | Butter |
| 45g (1.5 oz) | Blue Cheese (President brand) |
| 15g (1/2 oz) | Bread Crumbs |
| 45ml 1.5 oz) | Red Wine, dry |
| 1/2 t | Lovage, dried (see notes below) |

## CHOICE OF BLUE CHEESE

I suggest using a mild blue cheese here so that it doesn't overwhelm the steak. President brand Le Bleu is ideal in my opinion, but you may feel differently, of course.

## ADDITIONAL TIPS

For optimum results, use a very good red wine. My first choice is a French Graves wine. One affordable example: Château de France, Coquillas rouge, Pessac-Léognan.

If you can't get Lovage, then substitute equal parts of dried celery and dried parsley. The filling can be made up to two days in advance if it is stored in the refrigerator. Then just cut the steak open, stuff it and cook it for a fast delivery time.

## PROCEDURE

1. Melt the butter in a medium nonstick skillet and sweat the shallots on a medium-low heat (#3 out of 10) for 4-5 minutes.

2. Add the Lovage (or celery and parsley, if you are substituting them). Stir, then add the red wine. Increase heat to medium (#5).

3. After about 5 minutes most of the liquid should have evaporated. Add the bread crumbs and turn off the heat completely. Stir until the bread crumbs have absorbed all of the liquid.

4. Transfer contents to a bowl and add the blue cheese while the mixture is still warm. This will help it to blend together better, since the heat will melt the cheese. Mix well. You can store the filling in the refrigerator now.

5. If you refrigerated the filling, microwave it back up until it is warm (not hot) before continuing. If you put a cold filling in the middle of the steak, the center will remain raw. If you put a very hot filling in the middle, the center will be tough. You want it warm to the touch.

6. For the stuffing of the steak, I refer you to the video if you don't already know how to do this. The cooking directions are also explained in the video, and follow the same rules outlined under *Steak Mastery* section that begins on page 182.

---

DON'T BE THIS KIND OF COOK...

*The worst thing about making a dish that your family loves is knowing that you're going to be asked to make it again.*

# BAVARIAN BLUE FROG LEGS
# (OR CHICKEN WINGS)

*This works perfectly well with chicken wings, too—as shown in my video on YouTube.*

700g (25 oz) Frog Legs or Chicken Wings
90ml (3 oz) Milk
120ml (4 oz) Chicken Stock
30g (1 oz) Butter
2 t Flour
2 Scallions (separate green and white parts) - chopped
36g (1.25 oz) Blue Cheese (mild)
3/4 t White Pepper, ground
2 t (10ml) Absinthe or Pernod
5 T Bread Crumbs, coarse (sourdough)

## BLUE CHEESE AND ABSINTHE

This is an example of *anti-resonant pairing* (see page 26). You can test this yourself by taking a small bite of blue cheese and then sipping a tiny bit of Absinthe or Pernod. You'll find they cancel each other out, but when cooked together they create a new flavor that is a more sophisticated and complex, as well as being milder.

## ADDITIONAL TIPS

You can make a sort of "reverse Buffalo wings" by serving barbecue sauce on the side for dipping, which is especially well suited to this if you are using chicken.

## PROCEDURE

1. Heat the butter in a saucepan and then add the white parts of the chopped scallions. Sweat them for 5 minutes on a medium heat.

2. Add the flour and stir. Continue cooking another 5 minutes. The heat is just below medium (#4 out of 10)

3. Add the absinthe. Cook another 3 minutes with stirring.

4. Add the milk and increase the heat to medium-high (#7 1/2 out of 10).

5. After about a minute it will start to thicken. Now whisk in the blue cheese, lowering the heat a little.

6. After the cheese is homogenous, whisk in the chicken stock and the ground white pepper. Continue simmering on a medium heat for about 15 minutes until it thickens. See video for how it should look.

7. Adjust salt to taste. Add the green parts of the chopped scallions.

8. Arrange the sectioned chicken wings or frog legs out and sprinkle with salt and then flour. Toss around a bit to coat evenly with the flour.

9. Deep fry the chicken or frog legs for 3-4 minutes at 175°C / 350°F.

10. Drain on paper towel, then toss with the sauce mixture to coat.

11. Add the bread crumbs and toss so that they stick to the chicken. They can be held at this stage for a while, if necessary.

12. Spread pieces out on a silicone mat on a baking sheet. Slide the tray under the broiler of your oven at a distance of about 15cm (6 inches) and cook until golden brown (about 8 minutes - but broilers vary).

# BRUSCHETTA OLIVERO

*In Russia it is very common to have Italian restaurants with a sushi menu. Almost none of these restaurants have a chef who is either Italian or Japanese, by the way. This recipe incorporates elements of Russian, Italian and Japanese dishes.. You can forget the toast if you prefer, and just eat it like Salad Olivier. This is also a useful and flavorful element for a more elaborate plating of salad ingredients or roasted vegetables.*

| | |
|---|---|
| 200g (7 oz) | Cardoon or Celery Root, peeled |
| 90g (3 oz) | Fire Roasted Red Peppers (see below) |
| 60g (2 oz) | Green Olives, pitted |
| 60g (2 oz) | Tomato, seeds and membrane removed |
| 60g (2 oz) | Mayonnaise |
| 45g (1.5 oz) | Salami, diced |
| 30g (1 oz) | Parmigiana Reggiano, grated |
| 2 T | Shallot, minced |
| 1 T | Parsley, fresh, minced |
| 3-4 leaves | Basil, fresh |
| 1/2 t | MSG (optional) |
| Bread, Olive Oil | |

## FIRE ROASTED RED PEPPERS

Although you can roast your own peppers, the kind that comes in a glass jar from Italy are better unless you actually grow your own peppers and roast them over coals. You can substitute half the amount of sun dried tomatoes in a pinch and the result will still be very good.

## CARDOON OR CELERY ROOT

Cardoons are better if you have a choice, but it is impossible to get in Russia and seldom seen in many other parts of the world where celery root (celeriac) is readily available. Do not substitute celery stalks.

## ADDITIONAL TIPS

Once you make the topping, you can store it in the refrigerator safely for several days. You can also grill the bread on one side first and store it separately in a sealed container in the refrigerator. This enables you to prepare these anytime quickly, and the flavor and texture are still very good (although not quite as good as when made fresh).

## PROCEDURE

1. Dice and boil the cardoon or celery root in salted water until soft. Drain and cool to room temperature before proceeding.

2. Dice the roasted red peppers and the tomatoes. Slice the green olives in thirds.

3. Combine all of the ingredients <u>except the basil</u> in a bowl and mix well. You can cut it up further with a food processor at this point, and if you have not diced everything finely, that's what you should do. If you are a professional and going for a good looking presentation, then don't use a food processor. Just cut everything perfectly by hand.

4. Slice the bread and brush each slice with olive oil, or rendered bacon fat if you prefer. Either cook on a hot grill pan on the stove, or over coals. Toast both sides Obviously the latter is going to be better.

5. Mound some of the topping on the opposite (non-grilled) side of the bread slices. Put on a baking tray and cook under the broiler until the topping just starts to turn golden. The exact time will vary with your broiler, but keep the distance from the heat source to about 12cm (5 inches).

6. Cut the basil into a chiffonade for a garnish. Also add a little freshly ground black pepper. Some diced fresh tomatoes and a drizzle of olive oil are also simple touches that will enhance your presentation of this.

# EDWARDIAN CHICKEN CURRY
## (OR FOR QUAIL)

*This also works great on quail (see notes below). The origin of this recipe was the package directions from a circa 1910 bottle of "Chicken Curry Powder" that I found for sale in an antique shop. I improved it by replacing the dried cilantro and powdered garlic and ginger that had been part of the original spice mixture with fresh ingredients.*

| | |
|---|---|
| 800g (28 oz) | Chicken, boneless skin-on legs and thighs |
| 30g (1 oz) | Ketchup |
| 30g (1 oz) | Butter, melted |
| 25g (0.9 oz) | Garlic |
| 15g (0.5 oz) | Ginger, peeled |
| 1 T | Mango Chutney |
| 2 t | Chicken Curry Powder (see notes below) |
| 10g (0.3 oz) | Cilantro, stems |
| 1 1/2 t | Salt, preferably smoked salt |
| 400g (14 oz) | Onions, thinly sliced |
| Additional butter or ghee for frying the onions | |

## SPECIAL CURRY POWDER

See page 196 for how to prepare this. You may substitute a commercial Madras curry powder, but the results will not be nearly as good. I have left out ingredients from the curry seasoning so that I could replace them with fresh ingredients instead. Specifically, the dried ginger, garlic powder and dried cilantro. The original seasoning mix was combined with only ketchup and butter and didn't require a stick blender, obviously.

## PROCEDURE

1. Combine all ingredients except the chicken using a stick blender (or if you are scaling this up several times, then a regular blender.

2. Arrange boneless skin-on leg and thigh chicken pieces on a baking sheet, or (better) on a wire rack over a baking tray, skin-side down. Coat the meat side of the chicken pieces with the mixture. Allow to marinate for 30 minutes to an hour.

3. During this time begin frying the onions in butter or ghee until deeply caramelized. This will take 30-40 minutes on a medium-low heat.

4. Put the chicken in a preheated 210°C / 410°F oven with fan assist ON for about 16-19 minutes. If you don't have fan assist then increase the temperature by 10 degrees and the time by about 2 minutes.

5. At this point you can store the chicken pieces and the fried onions in the refrigerator and finish up servings any time. To finish the dish, heat a nonstick pan on the top of the stove and fry the chicken skin-side down to crisp it up some while you it is being warmed. When it is close to being done, add some of the previously fried onion to the pan so that can warm up, too.

6. Serve with rice, garnish with cilantro and mango chutney on the side.

If you have any difficulty, refer to the video on my channel *Crazy Easy Chicken Curry*.

## FOR QUAIL

Debone and coat the quail with the marinade. Let them stand at room temperature for about an hour before you either roast them in a hot oven, or (better) put them on a rotisserie over hot coals.

# EDWARDIAN FISH IN CURRY CREAM
## (OR SUBSTITUTE CHICKEN)

*This was undoubtedly inspired by Goan fish curry recipes, but it is much milder and not sour—perfect for the English at this time in history, as well as for novices first experiencing Indian flavors..*

| | |
|---|---|
| 350g (12.3 oz) | Fish (anything white and firm) |
| 30g (1 oz) | Ketchup |
| 45g (1.5 oz) | Onions |
| 22g (0.8 oz) | Butter, melted |
| 2 cloves | Garlic, minced |
| 1 T | Fish Curry Powder (see notes below) |
| 60ml (2 oz) | Cream, light (20% fat) |
| 1 T | Cilantro, minced |
| 3/4 t | Salt |
| a little | Lemon Juice, fresh |

## EDWARDIAN FISH CURRY POWDER

See page 197 for how to prepare this. As with the Edwardian Chicken Curry recipe, I have left out ingredients from the curry seasoning so that I could replace them with fresh ingredients instead. Specifically, the garlic powder and dried cilantro. The original seasoning mix was combined with only ketchup and butter, making Indian cuisine available to all.

## ADDITIONAL TIPS

This recipe also works nicely with boneless, skinless chicken thighs or leg meat. You can make this with chicken breast pieces, but you will need to pound them well between sheets of cling film so that they are tender.

## PROCEDURE

1. Combine the ketchup, melted butter, garlic and curry powder.

2. Mix this with the fish, coating evenly. Load this into an ovenproof dish and roast at 200°C / 390°F for 16 minutes (or 30 minutes for chicken).

3. Remove and allow to stand for 10 minutes for juices to run off. Meanwhile, slice the onion thinly and fry in a mix of butter and vegetable oil until golden.

4. Pour off the juices from the roasting pan into the pan with the onions cooking. Cook until it becomes thick.

5. Lower the heat slightly and add the cream and the salt. Stir until this begins to thicken.

6. Now add the fish to warm through, being careful not to overcook it. Add the cilantro.

7. Serve on rice and add a little lemon juice. This goes well with chapati bread, but naan is not as well suited.

> ### DON'T BE THIS KIND OF COOK...
>
> *By the time I make a list, go to the store to get the ingredients, come home and cook the food, serve it and then clean up afterwards, I could have eaten to McDonalds four or five times.*

# STARLIGHT MEATBALLS

*I developed this recipe at a restaurant that had an outdoor rooftop dining area. For some reason the decor featured an images of cherries. The two owners wanted some cherry dishes to tie in with the existing decor. This was offered as part of an appetizer course. The owners were divided. One said he didn't like it because he couldn't taste the cherries, and the turkey was like some other kind of game meat. The other owner argued that those reasons were exactly why he loved it—and he ordered this every single day, seven days a week for his lunch.*

| | SEASONING |
|---|---|
| 150g (5.3 oz) | Cherries, pitted and chopped up |
| 50-60g (2 oz) | Shallots, minced |
| 1-2 T | Vegetable Oil |
| 2 t | Sichuan Peppercorns, ground |
| 1 1/2 t | Salt |

## CHERRIES AND SICHUAN PEPPERCORNS

This is an example of *anti-resonant pairing* (see page 26). The resulting mixture has very little of the flavor you would expect, as strange as that may seem. It only vaguely tastes like either cherries or sichuan peppercorns. You must use sour cherries, though. Frozen are okay.

## ADDITIONAL TIPS

Frying the meatballs in unrefined sunflower oil gives a nice nutty aroma. This is an ingredient that you should acquire and experiment with. It is perfectly ordinary in Russia, but seldom seen in most western countries.

| | |
|---|---|
| 400g (14.1 oz) | Turkey Breast |
| 100g (3.5 oz) | Pork Belly (uncured non-smoked bacon) |
| 90g (3.2 oz) | Seasoning Mix (see previous page) |
| 45g (1.5 oz) | Bread Crumbs |
| 45ml (1.5 oz) | Cream |
| 30ml (1 oz) | Port or other sweet red wine |

Flour, Vegetable Oil (ideally unrefined Sunflower Oil)

## PROCEDURE

1. Heat a sauce pan or small stock pot on a high heat (#8 out of 10). Cook the shallots in vegetable oil for about 2 minutes until they start to brown.

2. Reduce the heat to medium-high (#6 out of 10) and add the cherries. If you are using frozen cherries, then let most of the moisture evaporate before continuing.

3. Add the ground Sichuan peppercorns and 1 1/2 teaspoons of salt. Continue cooking and stirring until it is nearly dry. Transfer to a bowl to cool. It should weigh about 120 grams (4.25 oz). Refrigerate while you continue.

4. Grind together the turkey and pork belly. If you are using pre-ground meats, then simply weigh the meats out. Don't bother mixing them.

5. In a mixing bowl combine the breadcrumbs, cream and cooled cherry mixture. Combine well before adding the ground meat. Now fold in the meat gently.

6. Form into meatballs. If you are making a soup with this, then form about 30 meatballs. Otherwise about 15 meatballs. Put on a plate and dust with flour. Jostle the plate to coat the meatballs evenly.

7. Brown them in vegetable oil, or (better) unrefined sunflower oil. Now mix the wine with an equal amount of water. Add to the pan and cover to steam the meatballs for another 5 minutes.

# LEMON BBQ SAUCE

*This is ideally suited to scallops or salmon that are grilled outdoors, but you can also use it on garlic chicken wings.*

| | |
|---|---|
| 300ml (10.6 oz) | Pear / Apple Juice Blend (100% juice) |
| 70g (2.5 oz) | Ketchup |
| 60g (2 oz) | Onion, sliced |
| 30g (1 oz) | Dark Brown Sugar, idealy Muscovado |
| 30g (1 oz) | Sugar, white |
| 30ml (1 oz) | Apple Cider Vinegar |
| 30g (1 oz) | Butter |
| 15g (0.5 oz) | Garlic cloves, crushed under back of knife |
| 1 whole | Red Serrano Chili, chopped |
| 1 whole | Dried Red Serrano Chili, crumbled |
| 1 1/2 T | Lemon Juice, fresh |
| 1 T | Liquid Smoke, ideally Mesquite |
| 1 t | Knorr Chicken Stock Gel (see below) |
| 1 t | Salt |
| 1 t | Turmeric |
| 1 t | Lemon Zest |
| 3/4 t | Thyme, dried |
| 1/2 t | Cinnamon, ground |
| 2 whole | Bay Leaves |

## PEAR / APPLE JUICE BLEND

Despite the strong citrus lemon taste, most of the flavor is derived from the reduction of pear and apple juice, so it is important to choose a quality product. Look for one that contains only pear and apple juices.

## ADDITIONAL TIPS

The use of the Knorr chicken stock gel is a shortcut that works well in most barbecue sauces because of the other strong flavors going on. You can use your own highly reduced chicken broth, if you prefer.

# PROCEDURE

1. Melt the butter in a sauce pan and begin sautéing the onions.

2. When they are soft, add the fresh and dried chili peppers, the turmeric, the cinnamon and the salt. Stir and cook on a medium heat for 2 minutes.

3. Add the dark brown sugar and the cider vinegar. Melt the sugar and cook until bubbling and sticky.

4. Add the pear/apple juice, ketchup, white sugar, garlic, Knorr chicken gel (or concentrated chicken stock, as previously explained), thyme and bay leaves. Bring to a simmer.

5. Cook at a simmer with occasional stirring. When reduced by about a quarter in volume, add the liquid smoke. Now use a stick blender to homogenize as much as possible. Continue reducing.

6. When it starts to thicken up, pass through a sieve two times into a bowl. Check the weight. It should be approximately 185 grams (6.4 oz). Return it to the stove (rinse out the sauce pan first).

7. If the weight was much more, then reduce it further to get it down to that weight. If it was lighter, then add a little water. When the weight is approximately right, add the lemon zest and simmer for 1 minute further.

8. Allow it to cool to room temperature. Stir in the lemon juice, bottle and refrigerate. Preferably make this up a day before you plan to use it to allow the flavors to mellow some.

9. Garnish finished dishes with sprigs of Lemon Verbena, if possible.

# PORT WINE BARBECUE SAUCE

*Although this sauce is ideally suited for game meats such as elk and venison, it can also be used on pork and chicken with great results. I don't recommend it for beef or seafood, though.*

| | |
|---|---|
| 150g (5.3 oz) | Onions |
| 500ml (17.6 oz) | Port Wine (see notes below) |
| 500ml (17.6 oz) | Apple Juice |
| 1 T | Cumin Seeds |
| 2 t | Oregano, dried |
| 1 whole | Red Serrano Chili |
| 1 whole | Ripe Poblano or Anaheim Chili |
| 1 whole | Dried Sweet Chili, or 1 T Paprika |
| 1 whole | Knorr Chicken Stock Gel Pack |
| | or homemade Chicken Stock (see below) |
| 22g (3/4 oz) | Garlic cloves, crushed with side of a knife |
| 1 | Cinnamon Stick |
| 150g (5.3 oz) | Ketchup |
| 45g (1.5 oz) | Dark Brown Sugar |
| 45g (1.5 oz) | Sugar, white |
| 120ml (4 oz) | Apple Cider Vinegar |
| 2 t | Liquid Smoke |

## PORT WINE

To make this the Rolls-Royce of BBQ sauces, use a great quality port, such as Taylor-Fladgate's 20 Year Tawny (or the 10 year to save some). To make this economical (as in for restaurant use), use a semi-sweet red wine such as Domaines Arnaud Cuvée Spéciale (France) and double the white sugar to 90g (3 oz). The result will not be as deep or rich, but it will cost a small fraction of the price. Beware of substituting cheap port wines, though. Many do not cook down well. A good quality semi-sweet red wine plus some sugar is always better than a cheap port wine in cooking.

## ADDITIONAL TIPS

Regarding the dried sweet chili, refer to Volume 1 of this series for a complete explanation. From a practical point of view, I suggest using the Knorr Chicken Stock gel pack. The result will be excellent. However, you can also substitute chicken stock, as stated in the ingredients. If you are doing that, then first reduce 500ml (18 oz) homemade low-sodium chicken stock down to about 100ml (3 oz) in volume and use that.

## PROCEDURE

1. In a dry pan (no oil) cook the onion on a medium-high heat to singe it. Take it to the point where it is nearly burning. Do not use a Teflon or other nonstick pan for this.

2. Deglaze with the port wine. Bring to a simmer to evaporate some of the alcohol before proceeding.

3. Add the apple juice and all of the other ingredients except only for the ketchup, sugar, vinegar and liquid smoke. Bring to a simmer for an hour.

4. Blend with a stick blender. Don't worry about making it a perfect purée.

5. Add the ketchup, sugar and vinegar. Continue cooking at a medium simmer for about an hour until thick.

6. Remove from heat and cool some before adding the liquid smoke.

7. Pass through a sieve. Bottle and store refrigerated.

# CHICKEN MARSALA

*This "classic Italian dish" is credited to English immigrants in Sicily, who also created Marsala itself by adding brandy to a local wine as a preservative against spoilage during sea transport.*

| | |
|---|---|
| 1 | Chicken Breast, large |
| 90g (3 oz)1 | Mushrooms |
| 2 cloves | Garlic, crushed with side of knife |
| 45g (1 1/2 oz) | Butter |
| 2 T | Flour |
| 3/4 t | Paprika |
| 3/4 t | Thyme, dried |
| 15ml (1 T) | Lemon Juice, fresh |
| 90ml (3 oz) | Marsala Wine |
| 1/4 t | Ajwain (optional) |
| Chives or Parsley to garnish (fresh), Olive Oil | |

## MARSALA WINE

Marsala has much in common with Madeira, but it is generally sweeter and has some complex herbal notes that Madeira lacks. The two are generally not interchangeable.

## ADDITIONAL TIPS

The ingredients and recipe shown here is for two portions. Scale it up by multiplying everything accordingly.

## PROCEDURE

1. Cut the edges off of the mushrooms to separate the pieces with the curved edges. Slice the rest into 2-3 flat-edged pieces (see the video if this is not clear).

2. Put the flat-edged slices into a bowl and toss with the tablespoon of lemon juice. Set aside.

3. Heat half of the butter (22 grams / 3/4 ounce) on a medium-high heat and cook the mushrooms and garlic for about 8 minutes. Remove from heat and allow to cool for a few minutes.

4. Drain the mushroom and garlic flavored butter from the pan into a tray you can use to dip the chicken breast pieces in.

5. Put the cooked mushrooms and garlic into the stick blender cup along with the Marsala wine. Blend until smooth. Set aside.

6. Combine the flour, paprika and thyme. Put into a plastic bag.

7. Slice the chicken breast through the thickest part and unfold the flap. Pound it gently between sheets of plastic wrap to a uniform thickness of 6 to 7mm (1/4 inch).

8. Dip in the flavored butter, then transfer to the back containing the flour and spices. Shake to coat evenly.

9. Fry chicken in olive oil on a medium heat. Add a little salt to one side as it cooks. Cook about 3 minutes on each side. If it isn't completely cooked through, don't worry because it will be cooked more in the sauce soon.

10. Add the other half of the butter (22g or 3/4 ounce) to the pan that the chicken was just cooked in. When it has foamed up, cook the sliced mushrooms in the pan. Scrape up any bits from the bottom of the pan.

11. Add the blended mixture of the Marsala with the cooked garlic and mushroom sides to the pan.

12. After a minute or two, the sauce will thicken up. Add the ajwain now, then the chicken back to the pan. Cook at a low heat (#3 out of 10) for about two minutes, then turn it over for another two minutes. Divide into portions and serve immediately with fresh parsley or chives as garnish.

# BEEF BOURGUIGNON II

*This is not the original classic version (my other recipe for this is), but it is easier and tastes at least as good.*

| | |
|---|---|
| 675g (24 oz) | Beef Loin |
| 120g (4 oz) | Onion, coarsely chopped |
| 120g (4 oz) | Carrot, cut into pieces |
| 200ml (7 oz) | Red Wine, dry |
| 45g (1 1/2 oz) | Tomato Purée |
| 22g (3/4 oz) | Butter |
| 22g (3/4 oz) | Olive Oil |
| 1 T | Flour |
| 1/2 t | Paprika |
| 1 t | Celery Leaves, dried |
| 1 whole head | Garlic |
| 1 | Bay Leaf |
| 2-3 T | Demi-glace (optional) |
| 1 full recipe | French Beef Stew Seasoning (page 198) |

## BEEF LOIN

Select beef that has some marbling, Remember to cut across the grain.

## PROCEDURE

1. Tenderize the beef with a Jaccard device along the edges, as shown in the video. If the meat seems especially tough, then cut slices and tenderize some more before finally cutting into 2.5 centimeter (1 inch) cubes, or a bit more. You may omit this step, but your result will be better like this.

2. Toss the meat with the seasoning mixture in a bowl. Then add the tablespoon of flour and mix some more to coat evenly.

3. Heat a large nonstick skillet on medium-high (#8) with the butter and the olive oil. When the butter foams add the meat in the pan. Brown lightly—enough to remove the pink, but take care not to burn the herbs!

4. Transfer the meat to a covered braising dish to wait. Add the onion and carrot to the same pan the meat was browned in. Don't stir too much so that they develop some good dark color on them.

5. Add the tomato purée and the paprika to the pan. Continue cooking until the wetness is gone (see video if you aren't sure).

6. Add the meat back to the skillet along with any juices that ran off. Also add 80ml (2.8 oz) of the wine and the dried celery leaves. Reduce the heat (#6) and cook with stirring until the wine has been reduced to a glaze.

7. Transfer the contents of the skillet back to the braising dish. Put the bay leaves on top and the head of garlic (slice the top off to expose the cloves). Braise at 155°C / 310°F for 2 1/2 to 3 hours.

8. OPTIONAL: If you would like to include mushrooms, fry them up in a skillet with some butter during this time. Add them to the braising dish about 30 minutes before the braise time is up, moving the head of garlic and bay leaves out of the way during the addition, then returning them.

9. Remove the head of garlic to a plate for now. Discard the bay leaves. Stir the contents of the braising dish and allow it to cool 15-20 minutes.

10. Lift the meat and vegetables out of the braising dish with a slotted spoon or spider. Set aside. Pour the liquid from the braising dish into a nonstick saucepan and add the rest of the wine to it (120ml / 4 oz). Pick the roasted cloves out of the garlic head and add those to the sauce, too. Add the demi-glace (if you are using it - but strongly recommended).

11. Heat the pan to reduce the sauce with occasional stirring. Continue until it reaches the consistency you prefer, as explained in the video. Now add salt (and MSG, if you want a professional result) to taste.

12. Pour the sauce back over the reserved meat and vegetables, then stir through gently. Plate up with fresh herbs. This is especially popular with fried potatoes as an accompaniment.

# BALINESE SPICY PORK

*This is very much like a pork version of the classic Indonesian dish, Beef Rendang. Nearly 90% of Indonesians do not eat pork because of their religion. Bali is the main exception, being primarily Hindu.*

| | |
|---|---|
| 700g (25 oz) | Pork Neck, boneless - preferably neck |
| 80g (2.8 oz) | Shallots |
| 60ml (2 oz) | Vegetable Oil |
| 5 whole | Red Serrano Chilies (see notes below) |
| 30ml (1 oz) | Lime Juice |
| 22g (0.8 oz) | Garlic |
| 22g (0.8 oz) | Lemongrass |
| 15g (0.5 oz) | Ginger |
| 1 T | Brown Sugar |
| 2 t | Salt |
| 1 1/2 t | Turmeric |
| 2 | Bay Leaves |

## RED CHILIES

This is intended to be a spicy hot dish, however much of the heat dissipates on cooking and storing, so even five who red serrano chilies are not overwhelming if you are used to spicy food. To make this more authentic, double the number of chilies. You can substitute Thai chilies, but don't substitute jalapeño chilies because the flavor is quite different.

## ADDITIONAL TIPS

Be sure to peel the tough outer layer of the lemongrass off before you slice it and grind it. Also note that the bay leaves are added later

# PROCEDURE

1. Trim and cut up the lemongrass into small pieces. Transfer all of the ingredients except the pork and the bay leaves into a blender and purée.

2. Pass mixture through a sieve. Reserve the solids - do not discard them.

3. Cube the meat up into 5cm (2 inch) cubes. Marinate in the liquid that passed through the sieve for at least 3 hours. Overnight is okay.

4. Thread meat onto skewers and either broil in the oven or cook over hot charcoal. Obviously the latter is better, if possible. If they are about 15cm (6 inches) from the broiler, they should take approximately 15 minutes of cooking. Then turn them over (as shown in the video) and given them another 4-5 minutes.

5. Tie up the solids from the sieve and the two bay leaves in a cheesecloth bag to use like a bouquet garni.

6. Take the broiled (or grilled) cubes of meat off of the skewers and load into a braising dish along with the solids tied in the cheesecloth. Add any leftover marinade to the braise, too. Braise for 2 hours at 160°C / 320°F.

7. Remove from the oven and allow to stand (covered) at room temperature for another hour.

8. Stir it around, then put the lid back on and allow it to stand for another 15-30 minutes.

9. It can be served directly at this point, garnished with sliced red chilies and cilantro leaves over rice. Alternatively, this can be mixed with a coconut curry sauce or cooked into a more complex rice dish, as you like. Prawns are often served with this.

# STEAK AU POIVRE

*This decadent recipe of steak, cream and cognac harkens from a bygone era when health concerns were not taken seriously. Still, every once in a while you should indulge yourself in the splendor of this dish.*

| | |
|---|---|
| 1 1/2 t | Black Peppercorns, whole |
| 3/4 t | Green Peppercorns, whole |
| 1/2-3/4 | Beef Stock Cube |
| 2-3 T | Demi-glace (optional) |
| 2 t | Worcestershire Sauce, Lea & Perrins |
| 30ml (1 oz) | Cognac |
| 70ml (2.5 oz) | Cream, heavy |
| 25g (3/4 oz) | Butter |
| 1 1/2 T | Shallots, chopped |
| 1/2 t | Parsley, dried |
| Olive Oil, Fresh Parsley for garnish | |

## STOCK CUBE

While purists may turn up their noses at the concept of using a manufactured ingredient such as a stock cube in a classic dish, the solitary goal of a chef is to produce the best flavor. If you have the sort of kitchen laboratory that Heston Blumenthal has, then you can prepare a powdered beef stock using a rotary evaporator under high vacuum. This equipment will cost you as much as a small automobile. Otherwise your best option is to use a top brand of stock cube like Knorr.

## ADDITIONAL TIPS

The addition of the homemade demi-glace will elevate this dish considerably. However, you can leave it out and still get good results.

An alternative method of preparing this is to use bottled or canned green peppercorns in brine. In that case you use only the black peppercorns in the seasoning mix and add about a teaspoon of the brined green peppercorns at the same time you add the demi-glace.

## PROCEDURE

1. Grind the stock cube with a mortar and pestle. Add the green and black peppercorns and crush. Don't grind them into a powder - leave some texture. Spread the resulting mixture out onto a plate.

2. Cut slices of short loin, or other cut of beef you want to use, about 1 centimeter (0.4 inches) thick and pound between sheets of plastic wrap until it is about half as thick..

3. Press into the spice mixture on one side only, because the meat is thin.

4. Rub the other side (not coated side) with olive oil.

5. Heat a heavy nonstick skillet to about 150°C / 300°F. Put the meat in, olive oil side down. You will cook the meat for about 3 minutes on this side, but...

6. After 2 minutes add the butter and the shallots to the pan. Swirl to make sure the shallots are in melted butter and not sitting on a dry pan.

7. Flip the meat over after another minute.

8. After about 30 seconds add the Worcestershire sauce and the cognac. Flambée, using due caution.

9. Remove meat to a platter after another minute. Now add the demi-glace and cream to the pan along with the dried parsley. Reduce heat to very low or off.

10. As soon as the sauce thickens in the pan, you are ready to plate it up. The traditional approach is to arrange the meat on a warm plate, cover with the sauce and add a little freshly chopped flat leaf parsley.

# CHICKEN LIVERS

*What you have to remember about liver is that it is loaded with powerful digestive enzymes that are reactive, especially at room temperature. They go to work digesting anything they come into contact with and the resulting products are usually not very tasty. Given the chance, liver will even digest itself to some extent. So the way to get the best flavor is to keep it cold, keep it away from other digestible substances, and cook it hot and fast to inactivate those enzymes. When these rules are followed the taste is entirely different from any liver you have probably ever had before. It is much milder and doesn't have any metallic overtones.*

| | |
|---|---|
| 250g (8.8 oz) | Chicken Livers |
| 30ml (1 oz) | Cognac |
| 15g (0.5 oz) | Duck Fat or Bacon Fat (or olive oil) |
| Ice Water | |
| Fresh Ground Black Pepper | |
| Fresh Sage (optional - see details in procedure) | |

## DUCK FAT OR BACON FAT

The difference is subtle, but duck fat will produce a more creamy texture, while bacon fat will contribute some smokiness, but tends to produce a slightly tougher outside edge. Olive oil is healthier, but it is not as good as either duck or bacon fat.

## ADDITIONAL TIPS

Trim aggressively! Chicken liver is not expensive. Removing the lobes completely and cleanly from the ligaments makes the final dish much more pleasant. You can fry up the ligaments separately as pet food, or if you are in a restaurant, grind them up as a component in sausage or hamburger.

## PROCEDURE

1. Wash livers in ice water. Trim off ligaments and cut large lobes in half. Transfer each finished piece to a bowl of ice water to hold while you continue with the rest.

2. Drain them from the ice water. Add the cognac and several twists of black pepper. Toss to coat evenly. Marinate for about 15 minutes before you begin heating the fat to cook them in.

3. Use a splatter guard over a heavy cast iron or nonstick pan. Heat whichever type of fat you are using until it is about 150°C / 300°F. You may also consider cooking matchstick-cut bacon initially to render the fat, and just leave it cooking with the liver to serve together. Add a little minced fresh sage at the end for the traditional French dish. A little minced shallot is also a welcome addition.

4. Drain the livers and pat them dry with paper towels, or a cloth towel that you will put in the wash immediately afterward.

5. Fry the livers in the fat, doing only a few at a time so as not to overcrowd the pan and lower the surface temperature too much. If you are going to use these as a component in another dish (such as the chicken livers in my recipe for Pasta Putanesca), then leave them quite rare because they will finish cooking in the sauce. Once they are cooked, most of the enzymes have been rendered inactive and they can be stored in the refrigerator for up to three days until needed without deteriorating.

# LOBSTER AND PAN-ROASTED VEGETABLE SALAD

*This is a dish that should have received more attention, but failed to capture the imagination of viewers on YouTube for some reason, which is a pity. I highly recommend this.*

| | |
|---|---|
| 120g (4.25 oz) | Potatoes, peeled and coarsely chopped |
| 120g (4.25 oz) | Carrots, peeled and coarsely chopped |
| 120g (4.25 oz) | Cauliflower, chopped |
| 30g (1 oz) | Onion |
| 2 T | Peas (optional) |
| 2 whole | Eggs |
| 60g (2 oz) | Bacon, lean |
| 30g (1 oz) | Butter |
| 90g (3 oz) | Crayfish or Lobster Meat, cooked |
| 1 T | Lemon Juice, fresh |
| 1/2 t | MSG (optional) |

Mayonnaise (to taste)
Fresh Dill and/or Parsley (as garnish)

## POTATO, CARROT AND CAULIFLOWER SCRAPS

This recipe is especially useful for using up end pieces of potatoes, carrots and cauliflower, which is always an issue in a restaurant where vegetables must be cut and trimmed for professional presentation. You do not *need* to use scraps here, of course!

## CRAYFISH OR LOBSTER

Whichever one you are using, be sure it is just slightly undercooked so that it remains tender after it has been cooked a bit more here.

# PROCEDURE

1. Boil the potatoes, carrots and cauliflower in salted water for 8-9 minutes until soft.

2. Drain on a colander and allow them to cool to room temperature.

3. Transfer the boiled vegetables to a food processor along with the onion, peas (if you are using them), and the eggs. Process to a chunky purée.

4. Cube up the bacon and fry it in a large nonstick pan on medium heat. Add a little oil, if necessary. Cook for about 10 minutes.

5. Increase heat to medium-high (#8 out of 10) and when the pan is hot, add the purée from the food processor. Begin cooking it like it was a potato pancake. When it starts to brown on the pan-side, begin turning it over and add the butter. See the video for how to do this. Lower the heat and continue cooking for about 15 minutes (again, see the video). As it gets close to being done, add salt and pepper to taste. White pepper is best.

6. Add the lemon juice to the crawfish tails or lobster meat. Mix and then add to the pan with the vegetables. Stir and cook for about 45 seconds.

7. Transfer to a bowl and leave to rest at room temperature for about 20 minutes. The residual heat will finish cooking the crawfish or lobster.

8. Refrigerate the bowl with the mixture until it is chilled, then carefully add the mayonnaise in a little at a time, tasting it. Also add the MSG at this point (if you are using it - and you should). Plate by shaping it with a ring mold and garnish with fresh herbs. This is an outstanding side dish for Lobster Thermidor.

# TOCHITURĂ

*The origin of this dish is Romania, but there are a great many versions in different regions and the surrounding countries. This is a version fit for a good restaurant or a very wealthy home. Often this is made this with only sausage, liver and pork kidney.*

| | |
|---|---|
| 300-400g (12 oz) | Pork (see below) |
| 4 | Pork Sausages, lightly smoked |
| 120g (4 oz) | Bacon, cut in four large pieces |
| 4-6 | Pork Ribs, smoked |
| 2-3 t | Paprika (see below) |
| 120g (4 oz) | Cherry Tomatoes, halved |
| 60g (2 oz) | Scallions, chopped |
| 90ml (3 oz) | White Wine, dry |
| 6 cloves | Garlic, coarsely chopped |
| 45g (1.5 oz) | Bacon Fat (or Duck Fat or Vegetable Oil) |

## PAPRIKA

Ideally you want to use the very large Romanian peppers shown in the video that you dried yourself and ground in a spice mill. Once you grind them they should be used within a month. If you can't do this, then you can use good quality paprika, but the results will not be quite as good. After all, the dominant flavor in this dish is the paprika, as you see.

## ADDITIONAL TIPS

Traditionally you would use a fatty pork cut like pork neck, but I chose medallions of pork tenderloin in the video to keep the dish from being greasy. If the fat content is not a concern for you, then increase the amount and use pork shoulder or neck for even better results.

## PROCEDURE

1. Heat the bacon fat (or other fat() in a 4 liter (4 quart) stockpot and add the bacon. Cook on a medium-low heat (#3 to 4 out of 10) for 7-8 minutes to lightly brown the bacon.

2. Add the paprika to the pan and stir for 20-30 seconds before adding the sliced pork. Lightly brown the pork.

3. Increase heat to medium (#5) and add the the cherry tomatoes and <u>half</u> of the scallions. Cook for 8-10 minutes with occasional stirring.

4. Add one clove of garlic together with the sausage. Cook for about 5 minutes with stirring.

5. Now you can remove the sausage and keep it aside so that it will look better in the final presentation, or leave it in the pot to have better flavor. It is up to you. Either way, now you add the smoked ribs and a liter (quart) of water. Bring to a simmer (#4 out of 10). Partially cover and cook for 1 to 1 1/2 hours, stirring about every 10-15 minutes.

6. Remove the lid and increase heat slightly to medium (#5). Continue reducing to thicken the mixture for about 1 1/2 hours.

7. Add the other 5 cloves of garlic. If you removed the sausages earlier, put them back in near the end of the reduction time (about an hour).

8. After about 5 minutes add the rest of the scallions and cook to the final thickness desired. Serve with polenta and fried egg, as shown in the video.

# SPICY KOREAN BBQ SAUCE

*This can be used as either a marinade for meats (especially beef and pork that will be grilled over charcoal) and as a sauce after the meat is cooked. You can also mix it with Bao Gochu Sigcho (page 81 of Volume 1) and a little white miso paste to make a great Korean salad dressing.*

| | |
|---|---|
| 200g (7 oz) | Pear, preferably Asian |
| 75ml (2.75 oz) | Soy Sauce |
| 4-5 cloves | Garlic, coarsely chopped |
| 2 t | Korean or Kashmiri Chili Powder |
| 1-2 | Red Serrano Chilies |
| 50g (1.75 oz) | Sugar, white |
| 2 T | Dark Brown Sugar |
| 1 T | Corn Starch |
| 2 t | Sesame Oil |
| 1/2 t | Black Pepper, ground |
| 200ml (7 oz) | Beef Broth (see note below) |
| 1 t | MSG (see note below) |
| 30ml (1 oz) | Apple Cider Vinegar |

## BEEF BROTH

Beef broth is not the same thing as beef stock. The main purpose of stock is to provide gelatine for body and an unctuous mouth feel. Broth adds a strong flavor of the meat itself. Broth can be served as a soup, while beef stock would not be a very good soup at all, having little taste. You can substitute a Knorr Beef gel pack (tub) for the broth, in which case you do not need to add the MSG called for here. In general, Knorr Beef and Chicken gel packs work very well in making most sauces and marinades. Of course homemade is better, but the savings in both time and money are immense, and the taste is indistinguishable to most people.

## PROCEDURE

1. Core and roughly chop the pear (including the skin).

2. Dissolve the corn starch in a small amount of cold water.

3. Combine all of the ingredients (including the corn starch slurry) <u>except</u> the apple cider vinegar in a sauce pan or small stock pot on the stove. Simmer for 30 minutes, stirring occasionally.

4. Remove from the heat and let cool for 5-10 minutes.

5. Purée until completely homogeneous. Use a stick blender for this quanity, or a large cocktail type blender if you are scaling this up.

6. Rub through a sieve.

7. Add the apple cider vinegar and store in a bottle in the refrigerator.

8. It will be ready for use the next day. The flavors need a little time to mellow. There are still chemical reactions taking place, even though you have stopped cooking it (as is almost always the case with foods). It can be kept in the freezer for months, but the best flavor is if you use it within two weeks.

DON'T BE THIS KIND OF COOK...

*I've had the same stove for ten years and I still don't know how to turn on the broiler. If it has one.*

# BEEF WITH ANARDANA AND MINT

*This is from the northeastern part of India where beef is eaten and anardana is popular. If you can roast the seasoned beef in a tandoor or over charcoal, so much the better.*

| | SPICE MIXTURE |
|---|---|
| 30g (1 oz) | Anardana |
| 2 t | Cumin Seeds |
| 2 t | Coriander Seeds |
| 5cm (2" ) | Cinnamon Stick |
| 1 | Dried Red Serrano Chili |
| 1/4 t | Mace (or 1/2 t Nutmeg) |
| 1-3 t | Kashmiri Chili Powder |

## ANARDANA

These is dried pomegranate seeds, and the key to this recipe is getting a good quality product. You cannot make them yourself effectively at home, and commercial products can sometimes be terrible. They should be slightly sticky (tacky) and have a pleasant aroma. If they are completely dry or smell like fungus, they are no good. East End is a good brand.

## PROCEDURE

1. Heat a cast iron pan until it is smoking hot (about 250°C / 500°F). Toast the anardana for about 30 seconds. See the video if this isn't clear.

2. Remove the anardana from the pan and add the cumin seeds, coriander seeds, cinnamon stick and dried red chili pepper to the same pan. Toast for about 45 seconds, shaking to keep from burning.

3. Cool the toasted spices. Put the anardana in an electric spice mill along with 2 teaspoons of coarse salt. After that has been ground, add the other toasted spices and grind. Add the mace (or nutmeg) and grind a bit more.

*152*

4. Rub the ground spices against a fine mesh sieve until you have 3 tablespoons passed through. Save the spices that did not pass through!

| | |
|---|---|
| 300-500g (14 oz) | Beef, cubed |
| 180g (6.3 oz) | Onion, sliced into rings |
| 22g (3/4 oz) | Garlic |
| 10g (1/3 oz) | Ginger, sliced |
| 300g (10.6 oz) | Tomatoes, canned |
| 30g (1 oz) | Ghee or clarified butter |
| 2 t | Coarse Salt |
| 1 T | Dark Brown Sugar (ideally Jaggery) |
| 6-10 | Mint Leaves, fresh (or more if you like it) |
| 1 t | Garam Masala (preferably homemade) |

5. Mix the Kasmiri chili powder in with the spice that passed through the sieve. Rub this spice mixture onto the beef and leave it stand for an hour.

6. Cook the seasoned beef in the ghee on a medium heat to the point that it is "rare" (5-6 minutes) taking care not to burn the spices on the surface. Alternatively, thread the cubes of beef onto skewers, brush lightly with oil or ghee and cook in a tandoor or over charcoal. This is much preferred.

7. Set the meat aside and add the onions to the same pan. Drain any juices that run off of the meat back into the pan with the onions while they cook.

8. After about 5 minutes add the garlic and ginger to the onions.

9. After about 2 minutes add the spices that didn't pass through the sieve.

10. After another minute add the tomatoes. Continue cooking on a medium (#5) heat about 25-30 minutes until very thick.

11. Add 300ml (7 oz) water and the mint. Stir and transfer to the cup of a stick blender. Purée until smooth and pass through a sieve. Transfer to the same pan (rinsed out first) and return to heat. Add the meat to the sauce.

12. Simmer on a very low heat for 2 1/2 hours, adding Garum Masala about midway. Then adjust salt to taste. Garnish with fresh mint.

# PORK (OR GOAT) METHI

*Many regional curry dishes in India do not have distinctive names. An American equivalent is meat loaf, which varies from cook to cook and also with regional influences, like cumin and hot chilies in a Texas meat loaf that won't be used in Minnesota.*

| | |
|---|---|
| 600g (1 1/3 lbs) | Pork or Goat meat, cubed |
| 30g (1 oz) | Ghee or clarified butter |
| 160g (5 1/2 oz) | Onion, sliced |
| 22g (3/4 oz) | Garlic, coarsely chopped |
| 2 to 6 whole | Green Seranno Chilies, fresh |
| 250g (9 oz) | Tomato Purée (pasata) |
| 20g (3/4 oz) | Cashews (or almonds) |
| 1 T | Coconut, dried (optional) |
| 2-3 t | Dried Fenugreek Leaves (Methi) |

## THE MEAT

Pork and goat are quite different in flavor, but this particular recipe is good with both. I do <u>not</u> suggest substituting beef or chicken.

| | SPICE <u>MIXTURE</u> |
|---|---|
| 2 t | Cumin Seeds |
| 1/2 t | Coriander Seeds |
| 1/2 t | Mustard Seeds |
| 1/2 t | Black Peppercorns |
| 5cm (2") | Cinnamon Stick, ideally true cinnamon |
| 1 t | Fenugreek Seeds |
| 1 t | Ginger, dry powder |
| 1 1/2 t | Brown Sugar, ideally Jaggery |
| 1 t | Red Pepper Flakes |
| 1/2 t | Citric Acid (optional) |
| 1 t | Salt |

# PROCEDURE

1. Toast the cashew nuts in a lightly oiled cast iron pan on a medium heat.

2. Set the nuts aside and lightly toast the fenugreek in the same pan, taking care not to burn it. About 30-40 seconds until darkened.

3. Wipe the pan dry and then add the cumin seeds, coriander seeds, mustard seeds, black peppercorns and cinnamon stick. Toast until the mustard seeds begin to pop (about 45 seconds to a minute).

4. Allow the toasted spices to cook before you grind them (including the fenugreek seeds, but _not_ the cashew nuts). Transfer to a bowl and mix together with the dark brown sugar, dried ginger, salt and citric acid.

5. Grind the cashew nuts next and put in a separate bowl. Reserve.

6. Put the meat in a bowl and rub with the spice mixture. If possible, leave the meat to stand for 45 minutes at room temperature.

7. Heat a large saucepan or small stock pot on a medium heat (#5 out of 10) and add the ghee or clarified butter and sliced onions to it.

8. After cooking for 5 minutes, add the meat to the pan. Cook with stirring for 4-5 minutes.

9. Add the garlic and the green chilies to the pan and continue stirring.

10. After a couple of minutes add the dried coconut if you are using it.

11. After another 2-3 minutes add the tomato purée (pasata). Stir and reduce the heat to medium-low (#3).

12. Simmer for 1 1/2 hours with occasional stirring. Scrape the bottom.

13. Add the ground cashew nuts and the fenugreek leaves. Stir again.

14. Put the lid back and simmer for another 1 to 1 1/2 hours.

Add a little freshly squeezed lemon juice when you are plating it. Be especially generous with the lemon if you didn't use the citric acid. Don't forget to add some of the _Hot Chili Oil_ to this (Volume 1, page 102), too.

# CABBAGE DUMPLINGS

*These are rather like a vegetarian version of French quenelles. They are especially convenient for being able to be prepared well in advance and finished up in a matter of minutes.*

| | |
|---|---|
| 180g (6.5 oz) | Cabbage, preferably parboiled |
| 45g (1.5 oz) | Shallot |
| 1 T | Butter |
| 60ml (2 oz) | Vermouth, dry |
| 30ml (1 oz) | Sherry, dry |
| 90ml (3 oz) | Water or Chicken Stock |
| 120g (4.25 oz) | Flour |
| 3/4 t | Paprika |
| 1 t | Garlic, chopped |
| 3/4 t | Caraway Seeds |
| 2 | Eggs (1 whole + 1 yolk) |
| 1 t | Salt |
| 1/4 to 1/2 t | Sugar |
| Vegetable oil | |

## DRY VERMOUTH AND SHERRY

The combination of dry vermouth and sherry in place of white wine is one of those old world chef tricks seen in fine dining restaurants long ago. Now it is largely forgotten, and it isn't even applicable to every recipe, but it is worthwhile here. You can substitute 90ml (3 oz) of a dry white wine if that's what you have on hand.

## ADDITIONAL TIPS

Chicken stock is also preferable here if you aren't trying to keep this strictly vegetarian. You can garnish these simply with a little fresh parsley, or (better) with diced grilled vegetables. Zucchini works especially well, but almost any medley of vegetables will go nicely.

# PROCEDURE

1. Chop the cabbage and the shallot up coarsely and fry in the butter plus a tablespoon of vegetable oil over a medium heat (#6 out of 10). Add the salt and the sugar. The sugar will help it to caramelize.

2. After a few minutes when a little color as developed on the cabbage, add the paprika and the caraway seeds. Stir and continue cooking.

3. After about 2 more minutes add the vermouth and sherry (or wine).

4. After 3-4 minutes more when it is mostly dry, add the water (or chicken stock) and continue cooking. You want it to reduce until it is nearly dry again, but this will take longer now as the cabbage begins to break down.

5. When it is nearly dry again, add the garlic. Stir and cook for another couple of minutes off the heat to soften the garlic.

6. Allow the mixture to cool a bit, then transfer it to the cup of a stick blender. Add the whole egg and the egg yolk and purée.

7. Scrape the mixture out into a bowl containing the flour. Gently fold into the flour. Mix only enough to bring the two together so that you have a light a fluffy dough. If you develop gluten, the dumplings will be tough.

8. Cover with a damp towel and let it rest for 20-30 minutes. Do not refrigerate, and do not let it rest much more than 30 minutes before you begin the next step. Get a pot of salted water simmering during this time.

9. Using two teaspoons, scrape balls of the dough into the simmering water a few at a time. After they float to the surface, continue cooking for another minute or two. Undercooked dumplings are gummy.

10. When you have accumulated a number of the dumplings in a bowl, add a little vegetable oil and shake to keep them from sticking together. You can store them in the refrigerator at this point for up to three days.

11. Put a few on a gratin dish, spoon over Béchamel or Mornay sauce and lightly brown under the broiler.

# DEEP FRIED PARSNIPS

*Parsnips are very popular in Britain, especially in stews and with roasted meats.*

| | |
|---|---|
| 2 | Parsnips |
| 90g (3 oz) | Bread Crumbs |
| 45g (1.5 oz) | Onion |
| 1/2 t White | Pepper, ground |
| Salt, Sugar, Egg, Milk | |
| Vegetable Oil for frying | |

## FREEZING TECHNIQUE

Slow freezing causes the formation of ice crystals that puncture cell membranes. As explained earlier in this book (page 11), this is what happenss in your home freezer. This is usually detrimental to the texture of foods, but in a few select instances such as this, it is actually beneficial.

## QUICK SAUCE

| | |
|---|---|
| 3 parts | Mayonnaise |
| 1 part | Ketchup |
| 1 part | Lemon Juice |
| Fresh | Thyme Leaves (no stems) |

Whisk together these ingredients to make a simple but quite complimentary sauce for these. Many restaurant "secret sauces" are nothing more than combinations of mayonnaise, ketchup, mustard and one or two other simple ingredients.

# PROCEDURE

1. Peel and slice the parsnips about 1.2cm (1/2 inch) thick.

2. In a pot on the stove, add the sliced parsnips to a liter (generous quart) of water with 2 tablespoons of salt and 1 tablespoon of sugar. Heat on high (#10 out of 10) until it starts to boil.

3. As soon as a boil is reached, put a lid on the pot and reduce the heat slightly (#8 out of 10) just to keep it from boiling over. Cook for 6 minutes.

4. Remove parsnip slices to a bowl and allow to rest until they reach room temperature (at least 30 minutes).

5. Put them in the freezer overnight. You can leave them for up to a couple of months if they are well sealed.

6. Defrost them at room temperature for at least 3 hours.

7. Toss parsnips with an excess of flour. Leave about 10 minutes.

8. In a food processor, grind the bread crumbs with the onion, white pepper and a teaspoon of salt.

9. In a bowl, beat the egg with a little milk.

10. Dip each parsnip slice in the beaten egg, then the bread crumbs. Press bread crumbs into the surface so that they stick well.

11. Deep fry pieces at 165°C (330°F) for about 5 minutes until golden brown.

# SPAGHETTI CARBONARA
# WITH SMOKY EGG YOLK

*The secret ingredient in this elegant version is the preparation of the baked and torched egg yolk that tops it.*

| | |
|---|---|
| 120g (4 oz) | Spaghetti |
| 4 whole | Eggs |
| 60g (2 oz) | Parmesan Cheese |
| 60g (2 oz) | Onions, diced fine |
| 60g (2 oz) | Pancetta, or Bacon cut in small squares |
| 1-2 T | Parsley, freshly minced |
| 1/2 t | Garlic Powder |
| 1/4 t | Smoked Salt (optional) |
| Flour for baking the eggs | |

## SMOKY EGG YOLKS

This is my own invention. Half of the egg is cooked in the shell, and the liquid part can be poured off, as you can see in the video.

## ADDITIONAL TIPS

When properly made, there is NO cream added to this dish. The key to a silky, creamy Carbonara is to add the egg to the pasta in batches, spaced out with pasta water. This is an instance, like risotto, where skilled home cooking will be superior to almost any restaurant, because a commercial kitchen can't tie up a cook and a space on the stove for 20 minutes to make one dish. Instead they add cream and cook it up quickly to get it out. The result is not nearly as good as making it like this.

# PROCEDURE

1. Fill a small ovenproof vessel with at least 5cm (2 inches) of flour. Bury eggs halfway into the flour with the thin end sticking up like carrots in a garden. Preheat oven to 150°C / 300°F.

2. Cook the spaghetti al dente in boiling salted water. Drain, reserving the pasta water. Toss the spaghetti with a little olive oil and set aside.

3. Put the eggs in the oven. Set timer for 30 minutes.

4. In a large skillet, gently fry the pancetta until it starts to become crisp. Remove it and set aside.

5. Fry the minced shallots gently in the fat rendered by the pancetta until they are translucent.

6. Whisk together the parmesan cheese with one egg and 90ml (3 oz) of the pasta water, which should have cooled down some by now.

7. Put the spaghetti into the pan with the shallots and heat. Toss with the parmesan/egg/pasta water mixture until it becomes creamy. Remove from heat and hold covered. Add more pasta water if necessary to keep it moist.

8. When the eggs in the oven are done, remove them to a strainer and run cool water over them for 30 seconds. Crack gently, discarding liquid white part. Set the cooked part on a plate to stand up. Sprinkle with smoked salt and then blister the top of the egg yolk with a blowtorch.

9. Plate up the Spaghetti Carbonara, adding a little freshly minced parsley. Now carefully scoop out the oven-baked eggs and place one on top of each serving, being careful not to let it break.

# HOT SMOKED SALMON WITH CRISPY GARLIC AND RED CHILIES

*Salmon is often prepared by cold smoking that we tend to forget how delicious it is hot smoked. The classic East meets West flavors (cumin, sesame, red chilies and garlic) play off of each other to create an altogether original flavor.*

| | |
|---|---|
| 600g (21 oz) | Salmon, cut in four filets |
| 2 t | Cumin Seeds |
| 2 t | Fennel Seeds |
| 2 t | Sesame Seeds |
| 3/4 t | Salt |
| 1/2 - 1 t | MSG (optional but strongly suggested) |
| 2-4 cloves | Garlic |
| 30g (1 oz) | Red Chilies, diced (see below) |
| 1 T | Butter |
| Fresh Herbs (for garnish) | |

## RED CHILIES

If you like very spicy food, then you can use Thai chilies, or even Habañero chilies. Generally I suggest a medium-hot chili for this, but there are so many different varieties in different parts of the world that you will have to decide for yourself from what you can get.

## ADDITIONAL TIPS

The MSG in this recipe plays an important role. Without it, the flavor is lacking and not as well balanced. It will still be good without it, but to make this really stand out, you need that strong umami note. If you are still afraid of MSG, please see pages 222-223 at the back of this book.

# PROCEDURE

1. Chop the garlic, but don't mince it too fine. Allow it to stand while you proceed with the next step. The reason for this is explained on page 51.

2. Heat a nonstick pan with about 20ml (3/4 oz) vegetable oil and gently fry the diced chilies for about 3 minutes on a medium heat.

3. Add the chopped garlic and the butter. Cook gently for about 5-6 minutes until the pieces of chili pepper are crisp.

4. Strain through a sieve. Reserve both the fat that is strained off and the chilies and garlic for later use.

5. Toast the cumin seeds on a very hot pan (preferably cast iron) for about 30 seconds. Then toast the fennel seeds in the same pan for 10-15 seconds.

6. After the spices cool down (3 minutes minimum) transfer to a spice mill along with the sesame seeds, salt and MSG. Grind to a powder.

7. Brush the salmon filets with the butter you drained from the chilies and garlic on both sides. Then sprinkle with the spice mixture on one side.

8. Load the stove top smoker with 1 - 1 1/2 teaspoons of wood chips. I use cherry wood for this, but it isn't critical. Put the salmon in and leave the lid open just a little.

9. Put the smoker on the stove and heat on maximum.

10. As soon as smoke comes out of the opening, slide the lid closed and reduce the heat to medium (#6 out of 10). Set a timer for 16 minutes.

11. Remove the stove top smoker from the heat, but leave it closed for another 2-3 minutes.

12. Take the salmon out while it is still warm. Divide the chilies and garlic up over the top. Drizzle with the remaining butter that you strained from the chilies and garlic, then add some sprigs of fresh herbs. Serve with a slice of lemon. Typically you would serve this on top of something else, such as pasta or with a fennel salad.

✦

# SWEDISH PLANKA

*The name is from the large wooden plank that this is traditionally served on. Although there is a version made with salmon, pork is the classic. Recipes vary wildly. This version is more complex and involved than any other I have seen, but it is also the best, delivering incredibly rich flavor that will have you making this dish again, despite it being slightly involved.*

| | |
|---|---|
| 85g (3 oz) | Mushrooms |
| 85g (3 oz) | Carrots, peeled |
| 400ml (14 oz) | Red Wine, dry |
| 50ml (1.75 oz) | Port wine (see note below) |
| 60g (2 oz) | Tomato Purée (pasata) |
| 2 | Bay Leaves |
| 1/2 t | Black Peppercorns |
| 6 | Juniper Berries |
| 1/2 t | Thyme, dried |
| 4 cloves | Garlic, peeled and chopped |
| 22g (3/4 oz) | Vegetable Oil |
| 15g | Butter |

## PORT WINE

Port wine will produce a better result, but if you want to cut corners you can substitute 50ml (1.75 oz) of red wine and 5g (0.2 oz) sugar. For more on this, see the section on Port Wine on page 134.

## NOTE

At the time of publication of this book there is no video for this recipe, but it will be put up on YouTube in the near future, including directions for preparing the Duchess Potatoes. Really the only difficult part of this recipe is making the marinade, which is described ahead.

## PROCEDURE

1. Cut the mushrooms and carrots into small dice, or grind in a food processor. If you are using a food processor, use it in pulses - don't turn it into a purée.

2. Heat a 2 to 4 liter (2 - 4 quart) sauce pan on a medium high heat (#8 out of 10). When it is hot, add the vegeteable oil. Wait 30 seconds for the oil to get hot.

3. Add the finely chopped mushrooms and carrots. Cook with occasional stirring for about 4 minutes. Get the smaller mushroom pieces right to the edge of burning without actually burning.

4. Add the tomato purée. Stir and cook for 30 seconds.

5. Add the red wint. Stir to deglaze, then add the bay leaves, black peppercorns, juniper berries, thyme and garlic. Bring to a boil.

6. Reduce the heat to medium-low (#3 out of 10). Continue simmering slowly for about 45 minutes.

7. Add the port wine. Cook about 5 minutes to reduce the alcohol.

8. Pass through a sieve, pressing down to get as much of the liquid as you can squeezed out. Even better, use the medium-fine plate of a food mill (pages 51-52) to extract as much flavor as you can from.

9. Cook either slices of pork tenderloin or beef filet mignon by searing them in a hot pan, turning over, adding butter and finishing in the oven. Then put the meat in a shallow container with this marinade ( single layer) right away, while the meat is still hot. Refrigerate, turning the meat over in the marinade every 6-10 hours for 2 or 3 days.

10. Remove the meat. Strain the marinade into a small saucepan. Add the butter and simmer to reduce until glossy. Gently reheat the meat in the sauce. Serve with duchess potatoes and sauce Bearnaise, as well as either asparagus or green beans wrapped in bacon.

# MEAT FOR ENCHILADAS CENTENARIA

*Inspired by the nearly century old menu favorite, "Enchilada Howard" at El Coyote in Hollywood. Anyone who enjoys Mexican food is certain to love this.*

| | |
|---|---|
| 800g (28 oz) | Beef Brisket, or Pork |
| 2 whole | Dried Red Serrano Chilie |
| 2 whole | Dried Green Serrano Chilies |
| 2 T | Oregano, dried (divided in 2 parts) |
| 1 T | Cumin Seeds |
| 1 1/4 t | Coarse Salt |
| 1 t | Kashmiri Chili or a Chile de Arbol |
| 1 t | Cinnamon, ground |
| 3/4 t | Garlic Powder |
| 3/4 t | Turmeric |
| 1/2 t | Black Peppercorns |
| 30ml (1 oz) | Tequila, Añejo |
| 200g (7 oz) | Onion |
| 150g (5 oz) | Tomato Purée (pasata) |
| 1 whole | Red Serrano Chili, fresh |
| 5-6 cloves | Garlic |
| 120g (4.25 oz) | Bacon, cut into small strips |
| Vegetable Oil, Cilantro | |

## BLEND OF CHILI PEPPERS

The key to this dish is the blend of chili peppers. Although Kashmiri Chilies are from India, the flavor works perfectly here. Alternatively you can use one dried Chile de Árbol pepper.

## ADDITIONAL TIPS

Ground cinnamon loses its potency quite rapidly. The amount specified here (1 teaspoon) assumes that you are not using a freshly opened bottle. If you are, reduce it to 3/4 teaspoon.

## PROCEDURE

1. Grind the dried chilies with 1 1/2 teaspoons of the oregano, the cumin seeds, cinnamon, chili powder, garlic powder, turmeric and coarse salt.

2. Coat the cubes of meat with the seasoning mixture and allow to stand at room temperature for 30-60 minutes.

3. In the bottom of a pressure cooker, brown the meat in vegetable oil, working in batches so as not to over crowd the pan. Alternatively, oil the meat and grill it over an open fire for even better results.

4. After you have removed the last of the meat from the hot pan, add the onion to it. When softened (3-4 minutes), add the fresh red serrano chili and the garlic. Cook another 3 minutes.

5. Add the tomato purée, tequila, and the rest of the oregano. Cook until thick (about 8 minutes).

6. Add the meat back to the pan along with 200ml (7 oz) water. Mix well, then put the lid on the pressure cooker and begin heating on high.

7. When the pressure release point hits, reduce the heat to very low and cook for 2 hours, keeping it just below the point where steam is released.

8. Increase the heat to medium-high so that steam begins venting and cook another 15 minutes. Release pressure and check to see if it is thick. If not, return lid and continue cooking another few minutes at full pressure.

9. Allow contents to cool to room temperature, then put into a container and refrigerate overnight.

10. Work in two batches using a large (28cm) nonstick skillet. Cook half of the bacon to render the fat, then fry half of the meat in the pan with the bacon until it is mahogany in color and flavorful. Set aside and repeat with the other half of the bacon and meat. Adjust salt to taste. You now have the finished meat for the dish. Serve it with fresh cilantro.

# CHEESE ENCHILADAS

*This is virtually identical to the cheese enchiladas as they have been served at El Coyote in Hollywood for nearly a century, passed on to me directly by the head chef there. The only difference is that they dip the tortillas in simmering pork lard instead of dipping them in the sauce. The pork fat method is the traditional Mexican way, but obviously less healthy.*

| | |
|---|---|
| 600g (21 oz) | Tomato Purée (pasata) |
| 600ml (21 oz) | Water |
| 2 T | Flour |
| 2 T | Oregano, dried |
| 4 t | Cocoa Powder, unsweetened |
| 4 t | Chili Powder |
| 2 t | Garlic Powder |
| 2 1/2 t | Salt |
| 4 t | Cumin, ground |
| 8 | Flour Tortillas |
| Jack Cheese, grated | |
| Cheddar Cheese, grated | |
| Onion, diced fine | |
| Scallions | |

## ENCHILADA SAUCE

This is an outstanding and simple sauce to make. If you can use ground dried Ancho chilies instead of the chili powder, so much the better.

## ADDITIONAL TIPS

If you are going to make these by dipping the tortillas in pork fat instead of the sauce, which is the traditional method, then do NOT dilute the enchilada sauce. Simply pour it over the top of the tortillas before baking them.

# PROCEDURE

1. In a large saucepan whisk together the tomato purée, water, flour, oregano, cocoa powder, chili powder, garlic powder and salt. Bring to a simmer.

2. After 30 minutes of simmering with occasional stirring, add the ground cumin and continue simmering for another 10-15 minutes. The sauce should be very thick now.

3. Weigh the sauce and add enough water to bring it up to 1.2 kilograms (42 ounces). You can store the sauce for up to three days at this point.

4. Heat the sauce in a large skillet until it is almost at a simmer.

5. One at a time, dip the tortillas into the sauce, then lay on a plate and add about a tablespoon of finely diced onion and a mixture of 2 parts of Cheddar cheese to 1 part of Monterrey Jack. You can include the meat from the previous recipe in this book, if desired. The amount of cheese and meat you add is up to you. Fold and put into an ovenproof casserole dish, as shown in the video for this recipe.

6. Spoon the rest of the sauce from the pan over the top of the enchiladas and then top with more grated cheddar cheese.

7. Bake for 16-18 minutes at 200°C / 400°F.

8. Garnish with freshly minced scallions.

# HALÁSZLÉ
# HUNGARIAN FISHERMAN'S SOUP

*The second most famous dish of Hungary.*

| | |
|---|---|
| 700-800g (26 oz) | Fish, freshwater |
| 2 T plus 1 t | Paprika (see notes below) |
| 140g (5 oz) | Onions, diced |
| 1 whole | Red Chili, fresh - moderately hot |
| 60g (2 oz) | Tomato Purée (pasata) |
| 1-2 | Bay Leaves, depending on size |
| 3-4 branches | Fresh Thyme, or 1 t dried |
| 1/2 t | Coriander Seeds |
| 45g (1 1/2 oz) | Rice (see notes below) |

Vegetable Oil, Salt, Pepper
Fresh Thyme leaves to garnish, ideally

## PAPRIKA

Although I use three different types of paprika, you can make it using only a single variety. Namely, a high quality hot Hungarian paprika. Be aware that paprika deteriorates with age fairly rapidly, and the best taste will only be obtained with the freshest ingredients. I don't usually emphasize the need for freshness, but it is a huge factor in this dish.

## ADDITIONAL TIPS

You can add rice, pasta or the traditional Hungarian *csipetke* dumplings that I showed in my Hungarian Goulash (Volume 1, page 94).

## PROCEDURE

1. Filet the fish. Set the deboned filets in a closed container in the refrigerator while you continue working.

2. Sweat the diced onions in about 20ml (3/4 oz.) vegetable oil.

3. After 3-4 minutes add the bay leave and first tablespoon of paprika. If you are using three different types of paprika, as I do, then this is when you add the hot Hungarian one. Also add the coriander sees at this point.

4. Coarsely chop the fresh red chili pepper up and add that to the pot. Continue cooking on a medium heat for another two minutes.

5. Add the fish trimmings including the head back to the pot. Cover with 1200ml (42 oz) water. Add the thyme branches and bring to a simmer.

6. Once it actually is at a simmer, begin counting the time. Cook for one hour with occasional stirring.

7. Cool some then drain through a collander. Pick out any large pieces from the fish pulp. Pass the rest of the pulp through a food mill using the medium hole size plate.

8. Rinse out the pot, then return the fish stock you just prepared to the pan. Add the tomato purée, 3/4 teaspoon of salt and 1/4 teaspoon of ground black pepper. Now add the second tablespoon of paprika. If you are using different types of paprika, this is when you add the homemade one from drying and grinding your own chilies. More salt will be added later, to taste. Bring to a simmer.

9. Add the rice (or pasta, or csiptke, if you prefer. Simmer for 10 minutes.

10. Cube up the fish filets and add that to the soup along with the last teaspoon of paprika (a bright red Hungarian sweet one).

11. Simmer for 10-15 minutes to cook the fish. Serve and garnish with fresh thyme leaves.

# Sandwiches

One advantage of a sandwich—especially a wrap—is that it can enable you to serve something that is impossible to plate attractively due to the color or texture. Creating a sandwich is a useful tool to keep in mind.

## SOME FAMOUS SANDWICHES FROM AROUND THE WORLD

### The Gatsby Sandwich from South Africa
Fried Bologna, French Fries, Lettuce, Ketchup and Piri Hot Sauce served on a large soft roll

### The Döner Kebap from Turkey
Meat cooked on a vertical spit is served with Tomato, Onion, Pickles and Sumac wrapped in lavash or pita bread

### The Banh Mi Sandwich from Vietnam
Pork Sausage, Head Cheese, Liver Pâté, Carrot and Cucumber on a roll. This is a fusion dish due to French settlers in Vietnam.

### The Zapiekanka from Poland
Sautéed Mushrooms and Cheese on a Baguette that's broiled to melt the cheese, then Ketchup is liberally applied on top.

### The Choripan from Argentina
Chorizo Sausage on a roll with Chimichurri Sauce.

# TAPAS GRILLED CHEESE SANDWICH

*This is sort of a Spanish version of tomato soup with a grilled cheese sandwich because of the sofrito that's cooked into it.*

| | |
|---|---|
| 120g (4 1/4 oz) | Tomatoes |
| 30g (1 oz) | Onion |
| 2-3 cloves | Garlic |
| 2 | Bay Leaves |
| 1/2 - 1 | Red Serrano Chili (optional) |
| 1 t | Pimentón (Smoked Paprika) |
| 1 | Egg Yolk |

Bread, preferably sourdough
Manchego Cheese
Cabrales Cheese
Olive Oil

## THE CHEESE

This is ideal with Manchego and Cabrales (which are the two most famous cheeses from Spain) however you can substitute Provelone for the Manchego and a mild blue cheese for the Cabrales, and still have a good sandwich.

## ADDITIONAL TIPS

If you are making this with a panini press, or a waffle iron that has been equipped with flat plates for sandwiches, then you should still follow step 8 in the procedures before transferring to the sandwich press so that it is crunchy. The texture is part of what makes this great, and you won't get that if you just put the ingredients on the bread directly.

# PROCEDURE

1. First make the sofrito. Purée the tomatoes, onion, garlic and red chili pepper (if you are using it).

2. Heat 2 tablespoons of olive oil in a nonstick skillet over a medium-high heat (#7 out of 10). As soon as the oil is warm (not too hot), add the smoked paprika. Cook for a couple of minutes until the strong pungent aroma has mellowed.

3. Add the purée of tomatoes and onion, etc. and the bay leaves. Reduce the heat to medium (about #5 or 6) and fry the mixture in the olive oil

4. Continue cooking with occasional stirring until the mixture is quite thick. See the video for how this should look.

5. Increase the heat to fairly high (#8 out of 10) and add another tablespoon of olive oil. Fry the mixture with stirring for 2 more minutes.

6. Remove the bay leaves and transfer to a bowl. You can verify that you have cooked it enough by weight. It should be 50-60 grams (2 ounces).

7. Let the mixture cool, then add about 1/2 teaspoon salt and the egg yolk stir to make homogeneous. As long as you let the mixture cool well before you added the egg yolk, it can be refrigerated and left for up to 3 days.

8. Butter one side of the bread and put the slices on a nonstick pan with the butter-side up. Cook for several minutes to dry out and toast the unbuttered side. The butter on the top side should have melted by now.

9. Flip the pieces of bread over and coat one of the slices with some of the sofrito mixture, followed by the two cheeses. Put the other piece of bread on top to assemble the sandwich. Reduce heat to medium-low (#4).

10. Put a weight on top until the sandwich is finished cooking. You might need to flip it over and put the weight on the other side, too. I suggest serving this with some thinly sliced onions that have been soaked in ice water and some quality green olives.

$\bf +$

# ITALIAN EGGPLANT SANDWICH

*Here is another vegetarian recipe with universal appeal—even to dedicated carnivores. The flavor is not exactly what you would expect, as explained below.*

| | |
|---|---|
| about 250g | Eggplant, peeled and cut into 1cm (1/2") slices |
| 1 T | Marjoram, dried (see note below) |
| 1 t | Coarse Salt |
| 1/2 t | Paprika, preferably Italian Forté |
| 1/2 t | Black Peppercorns |
| 1/4 t | Garlic Powder |
| Olive Oil, extra-virgin | |
| Pesto or Basil (see notes below) | |
| Mozzarella, wet-packed | |
| Bread of your choice - fresh Foccacia works well | |

## EGGPLANT AND MARJORAM

There is some interesting molecular flavor chemistry between marjoram and eggplant cooked together, although you have to use quite a lot of marjoram to experience it, as is the case here. Although you can still taste the eggplant and marjoram in the background, you'll find that the dominant flavor is something completely new and hard to describe.

You can use fresh marjoram for this, but then you need to do a larger quanity because the olive oil needs to be blended with the leaves. In that case, multiply all of the ingredients by four except the marjoram. Blend about 15 grams (1/2 oz) marjoram leaves with the olive oil and ground spices after step 2 in the procedure below.

## PESTO OR BASIL

If you want to minimize calories, then use a chiffonade of fresh basil, but pesto will produce a better flavor, as you would expect.

# PROCEDURE

1. Peel and slice the eggplant 1 centimeter thick (just under 1/2 inch).

2. Grind up the dried marjoram with the salt, paprika, black peppercorns and garlic powder in an electric spice mill (see the table of contents under *Kitchen Gadgets* for why you are grinding the herbs). Mix together with 45ml (1.5 oz) of olive oil.

3. Toss the sliced eggplant with the olive oil mixture onto the eggplant and allow to stand for 30-60 minutes before proceeding.

4. Put a large nonstick pan on a medium heat (#5 out of 10). When it starts to get hot, put the eggplant slices in (single layer). Work in batches if you don't have a large enough pan, or use two pans on separate burners.

5. Cook the eggplant slices for about 10 minutes without turning them.

6. Turn them over and cook for another 7-8 minutes without moving.

7. Add enough olive oil to the pan to coat the bottom and then turn the eggplant pieces over. Keep cooking slowly at a medium heat (#4 to 5). Turn the pieces over occasionally and move them around to ensure even cooking. You'll notice that almost none of the oil you added to the pan is being absorbed. The oil is there as a medium for frying. Continue cooking slowly for about 15 minutes this way, being patient and attentive.

8. Remove the cooked eggplant slices to a plate and allow to cool. They can be be stored in the refrigerator for days at this point.

## SANDWICH ANATOMY

Put two slices of bread on a metal tray. Spread a little pesto on each slice. Add eggplant slices to one side and mozzarella to the other. Slide it under the salamander (or home broiler) until the mozzarella starts to melt and the bread is lightly toasted. If you opted for the basil, then mince some and put it on the sandwich now. Assemble and let cool a few minutes. This can be packed to go and eaten at room temperature later.

# SPICED BEEF & ARTICHOKE WRAP

*Although there is some work in preparing the "meatloaf" for this, once it is done you can make many sandwiches from it. If you like unique and strong flavors, this will probably be a big hit. This is a good example of how a sandwich can be used to disguise something that's impossible to plate attractively.*

| | |
|---|---|
| 270g (9.5 oz) | Ground Beef |
| 150g (5.3 oz) | Artichoke Hearts, canned |
| 50g (1.75 oz) | Onion, diced |
| 50g (1.75 oz) | Bacon, diced |
| 30g (1 oz) | Bread Crumbs |
| 15g (1/2 oz) | Celery, diced fine |
| 1 | Egg Yolk |
| 2 t | Tarragon, dried |
| 1 - 2 t | Crushed Red Pepper Flakes |
| 1/2 cube | Knorr Beef stock cube (or 1 teaspoon salt) |
| 1 t | Sugar (white) |
| 1/2 t | Black Peppercorns |
| 1/4 t | Rosemary, dried |

## PROCEDURE

1. Put the tarragon, red pepper flakes, beef stock cube, sugar, black peppercorns and rosemary into an electric spice mill. Grind to a powder.

2. Drain the artichoke hearts and coarsely chop them. Put them into a bowl and add the spices along with the onion, bacon, bread crumbs, celery and egg yolk. Mix thoroughly.

3. Now add the ground beef to the bowl and fold together gently.

4. Spread this out on an ovenproof ceramic dish measuring somewhere around 20 x 30cm (8 x 12 inches). Bake at 170°C / 340°F for 1 hour.

5. Cool down to room temperature before making wraps.

# SANDWICH ANATOMY

This is much better after it has been refrigerated overnight. Room temperature is best for serving it. I don't suggest eating this hot or even warm.

You can use pita bread, a flour tortilla or lavash. This is a very strong flavored "meatloaf", which makes it very economical (especially important for a restaurant). That is, you don't need very much of this for a sandwich. Use plenty of fresh lettuce and tomato. Also be generous with mayonnaise. You can add a little paprika (bittersweet paprika is especially good here - see page 23) and some kind of cheese. Muenster and Jack are both good choices. Swiss cheese takes it in a weird direction, but it's still good. I don't recommend cheddar or edam.

DON'T BE THIS KIND OF COOK...

*I read recipes like I read science fiction. Every time I get to the end I think to myself, "Well, that's never going to happen."*

# RUSSIAN TUNA SALAD SANDWICH

*The classic American version is made with canned tuna. In fact you can make this recipe with canned tuna, too. However, Russians are sensitive about canned fish products because they have a notoriously bad reputation, Canned fish can't be part of the menu of any restaurant that's even halfway decent. When the owners wanted to put Tuna Salad on the menu at one of the best restaurants in the city, my task was how to elevate it to a higher standard.*

| | |
|---|---|
| 200g (7 oz) | Tuna, fresh (see note below) |
| 45g (1.5 oz) | Celery |
| 30g (1 oz) | Shallots |
| 15g (1/2 oz) | Sundried Tomatoes |
| 15g (1/2 oz) | Dill Pickles |
| 120g (4.2 oz) | Mayonnaise |
| 1 t | Lemon Juice, fresh |
| 3-4 drops | Tabasco Sauce (optional) |
| 3/4 t | Smoked Paprika (Pimentón) |
| 1/2 t | MSG (optional) |
| 1/4 t | Black Pepper, finely ground |
| 1 T | Tarragon, fresh (see note below) |
| 1 T | Ketchup (see note below) |
| 1 t | Soy Sauce |
| 3/4 t | Liquid Smoke, ideally Mesquite |
| 1/2 t | Onion Powder |

## TUNA

You can substitute canned tuna, in which case you won't need the last four ingredients in the list above and you can skip to step 3 in the procedures that follow.

## TARRAGON

This is an instance where the fresh herb is much better. However, if you can't obtain fresh tarragon then substitute 1/2 teaspoon of the dried.

## PROCEDURE

1. Mix the ketchup, soy sauce, liquid smoke and onion powder together in a bowl. Put the tuna in the bowl and coat with the marinade. Let stand for 30 minutes.

2. Cook the tuna on a grill pan on the stove, or (better) over hot charcoal. How much you cook the tuna is up to you. I char it lightly on the outside and leave the center rare. Allow it to cool to room temperature before proceeding.

3. Cut the celery, shallots, sundried tomatoes and dill pickle into small dice. Mince the tarragon. Alternatively you can use a food processor, but the result tends to be rather paste-like. That's okay if you are making sandwiches, but it is unattractive if you are serving it on a plate directly.

4. Break up the tuna with a fork into small crumbles. Stir together with the vegetables, mayonnaise, lemon juice, smoked paprika, pepper, tarragon, Tabasco and MSG (if you are using them). Taste and add salt.

5. Refrigerate covered in cling film for at least an hour, and several hours is even better. Consume within 24 hours, ideally. Although American tuna sandwiches are nearly always served on white bread, this version is far better on <u>dark rye bread</u>. Give that a try and you'll see what I mean!

# Jaccard Blade Tenderizers

Although there are a number of different types of needle and blade tenderizers on the market, the undeniable king for hand-operated devices is the line produced by Jaccard. In case you are not already familiar with these, they consist of dozens of razor sharp blades on a retractable mechanism that pierce and cut meat fibers by pressing down on the handle, as shown here...

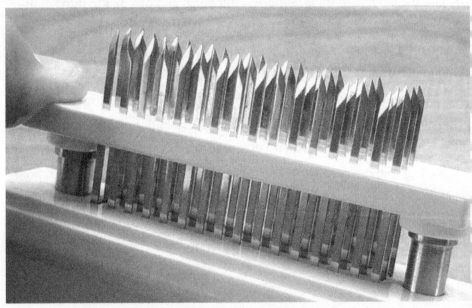

When used properly, this device can turn many less desirable cuts into seemingly top-notch steaks. The Jaccard comes in two basic models. One has a single row of blades and the other has three closely-spaced rows. A properly equipped kitchen will have both models because they serve two different purposes. The larger model is almost impossible to use on the sides of roasts and primal cuts—the blades get stuck and you have to wrestle with it to dislodge it after each stroke. On the other hand, smaller and thinner pieces are far more efficiently tenderized by the multiple rows of blades than by trying to use the single row over and over again.

## Does Jaccard Fail to Understand Their Own Device?

It seems perplexing that the directions and photos one sees explaining how to use the Jaccard device are almost invariably wrong. While stomping down on a cut in the direction that they show will result in some tenderization by separating fibers, this completely ignores the physical nature of the meat.

First you have to understand what makes meat chewy and tough in the first place. There are three factors: The diameter of the fibers, the length of the fibers, and the friction between the fibers (how tightly they are stuck to each other).

The first factor (the diameter of the fibers) is a matter of what cut of meat you buy. Filet mignon (tenderloin) has the finest grain, while brisket and shank have very coarse grain. No matter what you do, you can't make shank as tender as a filet mignon because the muscle is rich in connective tissues that won't break down in the short period of time that you cook a steak. Such cuts are only suitable for braising and for grinding into hamburger.

The cuts that you can make the best steaks from include the rib, short loin and sirloin. In order for a steak to be tender, the fibers must be as short as possible and to separate from each other as easily as possible. The latter is traditionally related to the amount and even distribution of fat marbling in the meat, because the fat melts quickly on cooking and acts as a lubricant to enables the muscle fibers to slide past each other when it is chewed. However, there is another way to accomplish this with less fat and less expensive cuts. I'll get to that in a minute. First, let's consider the other factor: The length of the fibers.

The direction of the grain in meat is the direction that the muscle fibers run in. To shorten these fibers, this is the direction you want to primarily apply the Jaccard device in. Although you can do it with single pre-cut steaks, it is easier to work with larger cuts along the sides before you slice them into steaks.

After you first cut a great many of the fibers into short bits by going in from the side, then you can also do some more tenderizing across the surface, as shown in the photo on the previous page. This is mostly important in regions of the meat that have heavy fat deposits, because the holes you poke will help the fat melt and run away easier, making for a better dining experience.

Now that you have mashed the meat from all sides, first with the single row of blades along the edges, and then with the triple-row model across the face and back of each steak, your meat looks a bit like road kill, but don't despair. Simply pull it away from the board and fluff it up in a similar way you would fluff up a pillow. You want to stand it up so that the fibers are running in the direction from the floor to the ceiling (or if you are grilling outdoors, from the earth to the sky). If the meat is more than about 2cm (3/4 inch) thick, tie a loop of twine around it to help it remain fluffed up during the cooking process.

Here is the real magic of the Jaccard device when it is properly used: When you put the meat down on the hot pan, steam is generated. That steam has to go somewhere, and you have

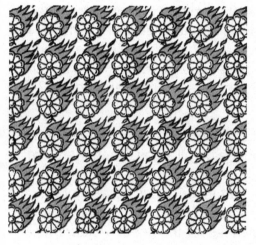

created a path between the fibers of the meat. Those cut fibers move out of the way of the steam, separating from each other. They don't have to be lubricated with heavy fat marbling—the force of the steam will pull them apart from each other. This effect only extends a short distance into the surface, but if the steak is not too thick and both sides of the meat have this treatment, only the center of each steak will have much friction between the fibers. We help that out further by putting some butter on top when it is turned, because now that the fibers have separated, the butter melts and can run down between them, creating the same effect as perfectly marbled meat, only with much less actual fat. The exact procedure will be described just ahead.

So, we are left with the puzzle as to why this is not the method that is generally shown to people—even by Jaccard themselves. I can think of several reasons, including the desire to make the device seem completely idiot proof, but still I think the most probable reason is the fear of lawsuits over sanitation issues...

## Sanitation Concerns

The one complaint that you hear about with all blade tenderizing devices (including Jaccard's) is the issue of sanitation. Once you use one, there are bacteria on the blades. They are dishwasher safe, so there is no excuse for putting the device back in your kitchen drawer without washing it properly. If you don't have a dishwasher, you can always mix up a weak bleach solution (about a tablespoon per liter of water) and soak the entire device in that for five minutes. Then rinse it off, and it will be as sterile, though not as physically clean as having been through a dishwasher.

This is not the only concern, though. The problem with all meat is that there are bacteria alive and growing on the exposed surfaces. The interior of beef is generally very safe and clean, but as soon as you grind or stab raw meat in any way, you are driving the bacteria from the surface down into the middle of the meat. The outside will be seared, even if you are going to serve it very rare, but the interior of the meat can be seriously contaminated if you used a tenderizer extensively. So, how do you get around this? There are three approaches...

The first is to cut a block out of a larger piece of meat so that you begin with clean exposed edges on all sides. Then there are almost no bacteria on the surface to be driven down into the interior. The problem with this is that it generates quite a lot of waste—meat that is going to be scraps for stock or ground into hamburger. This is an acceptable loss for the finest restaurants, where absolute safety for customers is paramount, and the square block-shaped pieces of meat can be plated attractively for an aesthetic advantage. Most home cooks are not so happy with this approach because it can effectively double the cost of the meat.

The second approach is to use a blowtorch on all of the exposed surfaces first. It only takes a few seconds to kill bacteria with a blowtorch—far less time than it takes to cook the meat. If you have a large piece of meat that you will be cutting several steaks from, then this is an attractive option because it won't take you long, and all of the internal surfaces are already safe when you slice them.

The third (and easiest) method is to simply not worry about it! However, if you have a restaurant with legal liability, this is out of the question. Nor would I advise you to ignore this potential health hazard and put myself at the risk of a lawsuit, either. What I can tell you is that many people who use blade tenderizers don't concern themselves with the increased concentration of *E. coli* in the middle of the meat because they either cook the meat until it reaches a safe internal temperature (rather than serving it rare), or they just have a good constitution and don't get sick from it anyway. Bear in mind that those at the greatest risk are small children and the elderly. The <u>safe</u> way to eat rare meat is to sanitize the outside first.

## Achieving Even Shorter Fibers for More Tenderness

Your final opportunity to turn a tough cut into a tender one lies in how the cooked steak is cut. By slicing it at a 45 degree angle to the surface, you are cutting the maximum number of fibers through the center (the ones that were not separated by the steam) as short as possible. Of course, most guests prefer to cut their own steak up, but to ensure that your family gets super tender meat, do the cutting for them in this manner. Just be sure to let the steak rest very well before cutting it, and use a very sharp knife.

*Slicing at a 45 degree angle to maximize tenderness.*

# The Sawtooth Steak Chart

On the opposite side of this page you will see a rather complex graph. Don't be intimidated, and if you cook steak on a regular basis, make a photocopy of this spread and keep it in your kitchen. Here's how it works:

Find the thickness of the steak you will be cooking along the bottom edge of the chart. Now follow that mark up to the sawtooth line and look to the left. This is the temperature you will sear the steak at. The point along the curved line is read on the right side. This is the number of minutes it will be in the oven after searing on one side in a hot pan.

---

## PROCEDURE

1. While the meat is still cold, trim and tenderize it (see previous section on Jaccard devices). Add coarse salt and coarse ground black pepper, then allow the steaks to stand at room temperature for about an hour.

2. Heat a heavy oven-proof pan (preferably cast iron) to the SEARING TEMPERATURE (left side of the chart) that matches the thickness of the meat you are cooking along the sawtooth line. An infrared surface-reading thermometer is ideal for this. Now blot the meat with paper towel and apply olive oil to it. Oil the meat, not the pan. Place steak in the pan. Do NOT crowd pan with multiple steaks, and do NOT move it until you are reasonably sure it is browned on that side. Lift a corner to check before flipping.

3. The moment you flip the meat in the pan, add a lump of butter to the top and transfer the pan to the oven (if it is over 1.3cm thick - see chart). Roast for the time indicated at the right edge of the chart along the curved line.

4. Remove from oven, flip meat to other side of pan. Wait 30 seconds. Transfer to a plate and allow to rest for 20 minutes or more. *"Better to reheat than to cut hot meat."*

---

Note that the oven times shown are for rare to medium-rare. For more well done cuts, increase the oven time. Medium-well is twice the time shown. The oven temperature is 170°C (340°F) until you get to a piece of

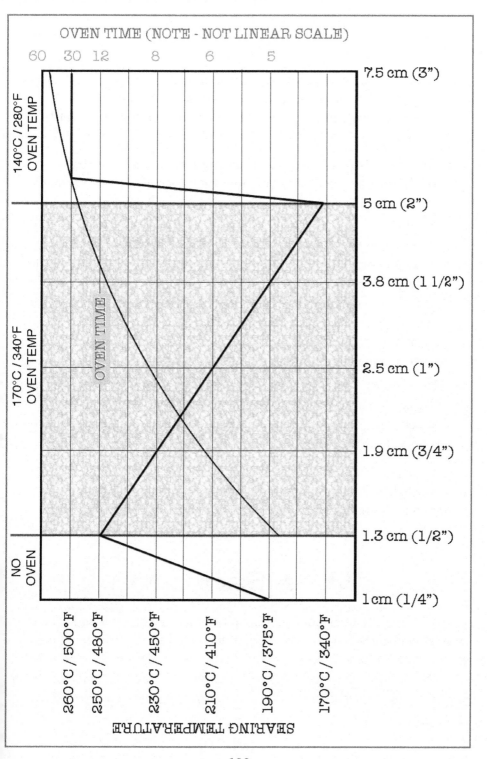

meat that's more than 5cm (2 inches) thick, at which point you have crossed over into a region that is more like cooking a roast, so the temperature from this point on is 140°C (280°F) to allow more time for deeper and gentler heat penetration. Note that the oven time on the right side of the graph is not linear; there is a sharp increase in time corresponding to the point where the oven temperature is lower (12 minutes jumps to 30 minutes suddenly.)

PAILLARD MODE (1.0 - 1.3cm) You are driving heat into the middle. It is an achievable goal to cook the interior at the same time the outside is seared. After searing one side, flip the meat to the other side of the pan and remove the pan from the heat. Let the residual heat of the metal cook the other side through.

STEAK MODE (1.3 - 5 cm) You are only warming the interior while you sear the outside. Thus, the thicker the piece of meat, the lower the searing temperature (this is counter-intuitive to most people). This makes the sear take longer, and thus gives more time for heat to penetrate to the depth of the interior. After searing on one side, transfer to the oven to finish.

ROAST BEEF MODE (5 cm and up) This can no longer be treated as a steak. You simply brown the outside quickly for the benefit of the flavorful Maillard reaction, and then slowly roast it in the oven to cook it through evenly.

The most difficult steaks to cook properly are 1.3cm and 5cm, because they are right on the cusp of two different techniques. Make your life easier by avoiding those two specific thicknesses whenever possible.

# More Seasoning

To really taste the meat itself, stick to simply coarse salt and coarse ground pepper. When you get tired of that plain vanilla approach, there are an unlimited number of marinades and dry rubs to experiment with. Even simpler, when you put the lump of butter on the steak, add sprigs of fresh herbs and/or a crushed clove of garlic before putting the pan in the oven.

# Spice Blends

NOTE: When making spice blends, put a label on the bottle with the date you ground them. Most blends should be used within a month unless otherwise noted.

## FOR EDGES OF GRILLED / ROASTED BEEF

Try rolling the outside fatty edge of steaks in some of this seasoning on a plate. Use only very lightly on the rest of the meat because this is a potent blend.. This is also excellent when applied to the fat cap of a standing rib roast before cooking. Apply it as soon as you take the meat out of refrigeration to warm to room temperature before cooking.

| | |
|---|---|
| 1 1/2 T | 4-Mix Peppercorns (black, white, green, pink) |
| 1 T | Garlic Powder |
| 1 1/2 t | Cumin Seeds |
| 1 1/2 t | Rosemary, dried |
| 1 1/2 t | Dried Tomatoes (see page 23) |
| 1/2 t | Basil, dried |
| 1/2 of a whole | Star Anise |
| 1/4 t | Cayenne |
| 1 T | Coarse Salt |

Grind all of the ingredients except the salt together in an electric spice mill. Now add the salt and pulse the motor a few times to create medium-grains of salt (larger than table salt, but smaller than kosher salt). Bottle and store in a cool, dark place. Ideally use this within a month.

# CHILI POWDER

Many people imagine that the bottled chili powder sold is simply ground up dried chilies. In fact it is an assortment of spices and generally not even very hot. The name is because it is the spice blend people use to make the popular American dish, *Chilli con Carne,* frequently known as simply Chilli.

In the same way that I suggest personalizing your liquors for cocktails in my *Cocktails of the South Pacific* book, the same is true here of Chili Powder. This is a potent and very flavorful blend that has little in common with the store bought product.

| | |
|---|---|
| 2 whole | Dried Sweet Red Chilies |
| 2 whole | Mulato Chilies (dried) |
| 1-3 whole | Dried Red Serrano Chilies |
| 1 t | Salt, coarse |
| 1 1/2 t | Oregano, dried |
| 1 1/2 t | Cumin Seeds |
| 1 t | Paprika, best quality (see page 23) |
| 1/2 t | Smoked Paprika (Pimentón) |
| 1/4 t | Cinnamon, ground |
| 1/4 t | Fennel Seeds |
| 4 whole | Cloves (the spice - not garlic) |
| 1/4 - 1/2 | Bay Leaf (depending on size) |

Put the dried chilies in an electric spice grinder with the coarse salt to begin with. Exactly how hot you want this will be determined by the number of dried red serrano chilies. For more about the types of dried chilies, see Volume 1 of this cookbook series. Add all of the rest of the ingredients and grind until as much of a powder as is possible. Store in an closed jar away from direct light. Ideally you want to use this within a month, but it will still be more flavorful than the commercial variety even six months later.

# "LSD" SEASONING 2

The name of this arose because it was initially composed of equal parts of Lovage, Salt and Dill. The list of ingredients expanded over the years as the recipe was refined.

| | |
|---|---|
| 2 t | Lovage, dried (see note below) |
| 2 t | Dill, dried |
| 1 t | Salt |
| 3/4 t | Onion Powder |
| 1/2 t | Thyme, dried |
| 1/2 t | Chili Powder (see note below) |
| 1/2 t | MSG |
| 1/4 t | Parsley, dried |
| 1/4 t | Tarragon, dried |
| 1/4 t | White Pepper, ground |

You can use a commercial chili powder for this, but the results will be even better if you use my mix from the previous page here. If you can't get dried lovage, then you can substitute equal parts of dried celery leaves and dried parsley (more dried parsley than it includes otherwise, that is). The result will not have the same magic that lovage brings, but it will still be good.

Combine all of the ingredients in an electric spice mill. Grind to a powder and store in a closed container away from direct light. This should be used within three months.

## FRENCH HERBS FROM LYON

While I generally discourage people from purchasing commercially manufactured blends of spices and herbs, the concept of having a single bottle mixture that can be dispensed in small portions is very practical. Think of it this way: Half a teaspoon of this mixture contains only a microscopic amount of the lesser ingredients, but the balance is still the same, so this sort of mixture takes on a life of its own.

| | |
|---|---|
| 2 1/2 t | Thyme, dried |
| 1 1/2 t | Tarragon, dried |
| 1 t | Chervil, dried |
| 1 t | Parsley, dried |
| 3/4 t | Chives, dried |
| 1/2 t | Rosemary, dried |
| 1/2 t | Celery Leaf, dried |
| 1/4 t | Marjoram, dried |
| 1/4 t | Lavender, culinary (optional) |

Whiz these up in a spice mill briefly just before using. Don't grind them all up ahead of time, or they will lose their potency quickly.. If you use lavender, be sure to obtain a culinary grade. The lavender you get from a florist contains pesticides, and it is also not nearly as potent as the culinary grade.

# DRY RUB FOR WHOLE ROTISSERIE STYLE CHICKEN

By now almost everyone has tasted those orange chickens that were cooked in a grocery store rotisserie oven. The idea is good, but usually poorly executed compared to what you can make yourself—and it is really easy. I know I've mentioned this before, but one of the big differences between restaurant and home cooking is the amount of seasoning used. On average I would say that a restaurant recipe contains about four times as much seasoning as a home recipe would call for. This is only enough for two small chickens. Put a good amount inside the cavity, too!

You can substitute a tablespoon of Knorr vegetable stock mix for the teaspoon each of onion powder, dried celery and dried carrot.

After evenly coating the chicken (don't forget to put some inside the

|  |  |
|---|---|
| 1 T | Paprika, best quality (see page 23) |
| 1/2 - 1 | Knorr Chicken Stock Cube, ground |
| 2 t | Dark Brown Sugar, preferably Cassonade |
| 1 t | Thyme, dried |
| 1 t | 4-Mix Peppercorns (black, white, green, pink) |
| 1 t | Onion Powder |
| 1 t | Dried Celery |
| 1 t | Dried Carrot |
| 1 t | Salt, coarse |
| 1/2 t | Oregano, dried |
| 1/2 t | Turmeric |
| 1/2 t | Citric Acid |
| 1/2 t | Garlic Powder |
| 1/2 t | Cayenne Pepper |

cavity), seal it up in a plastic back (vacuum sealing is even better) and refrigerate it for 1-2 days. Either cook it on a rotisserie, or roast it in the oven at 175°C (350°F) for about 1 1/2 hours (varies some with the size of the chicken). Let it cool for 45 minutes before cutting.

## EDWARDIAN CHICKEN CURRY SPICE MIX

The advantage to oven roasting the spices here is that they can be used directly on meat without the usual Indian method of toasting and then cooking in ghee with onions. The disadvantage is that once you prepare

| | |
|---|---|
| 3 t | Coriander Seeds |
| 2 1/2 t | Turmeric |
| 1 t | Black Peppercorns |
| 1/4 t | Cinnamon, ground |
| 1/4 t | Cumin Seeds |
| 5 whole | Green Cardamom pods |

this mixture, it has a relatively short shelf life. Try to use it within 2 weeks, and no more than a month. You can improve the life if you have a vacuum sealer, such as used in sous vide cooking. Sealed under vacuum and stored in the refrigerator (not the freezer) it can be kept for up to three months. Don't freeze spices.

Mix all of the ingredients in a ceramic or glass cup and cover with foil. Roast overnight at 80°C / 175°F (10-14 hours). Remove from the oven and let stand with the foil cover still on until it reaches room temperature.

Grind the spices that were roasted in an electric spice mill, then pass them through a fine mess sieve. Discard any solids that won't pass.

Make sure to write the date you prepared this on a label so you can keep track of how old it is.

# EDWARDIAN FISH CURRY SPICE MIX

This mixture includes the coconut, and there is some slight similarity to Tikka Masala, given the nutmeg and cardamom notes—especially if you use this for chicken instead of fish (see the index for the recipe).

| | |
|---|---|
| 2 t | Turmeric |
| 2 t | Cumin Seeds |
| 1 t | Coriander Seeds |
| 1/2 t | Kashmiri Chili Powder, or Cayenne |
| 1/2 t | Nutmeg, ground |
| 1/2 t | Ginger, ground |
| 1/4 t | Black Peppercorns |
| 1/4 t | Fenugreek, whole |
| 1/4 t | Asafoetida |
| 4 whole | Cloves (the spice) |
| 7 whole | Green Cardamom pods |
| 2 T | Coconut, dessicated (unsweetened) |
| 1 t | MSG (optioinal) |

Mix all of the ingredients except for the coconut in a ceramic cup and cover with foil. Roast overnight at 80°C / 175°F (10-14 hours). Remove from the oven and let stand with the foil cover still on until it reaches room temperature.

Toast the coconut on a dry pan over a medium heat. Try to get it all evenly brown, but not at all burnt. Grind the spices that were roasted in an electric spice mill along with the MSG (if you are using it), then pass them through a fine mess sieve. Discard any solids that won't pass. Now mix in the toasted coconut.

You can use it this way, but for better results, grind the spices with the coconut again and pass through a sieve once more. Passing it through the sieve the second time will be more difficult because of oil in the coconut, but then you will have a much smoother curry.

## FRENCH BEEF STEW SEASONING

Dried tomatoes have natural MSG in them. So does Parmesan cheese, which is why pizza is universally popular.

| | |
|---|---|
| 2 t | Dried Tomatoes |
| | or substitute 1 teaspoon each of Paprika and MSG |
| 1 1/2 t | Coarse Salt |
| 1 t | Green Peppercorns, dried |
| | or substitute 3/4 t Black Peppercorns |
| 1 t | Brown Sugar, ideally Cassonade |
| 1 t | Chives, dried |
| 1/2 t | Rosemary, dried |
| 1/2 t | Parsley, dried |
| 1/2 t | Tarragon, dried |
| 1/2 t | Chervil, dried |
| 1/2 t | Marjoram, dried |

Grind the dried tomatoes, coarse salt, peppercorns and brown sugar in an electric spice mill. Transfer to a bottle with a screw cap. Add all of the dried herbs. Put the cap on and shake to mix. Best when used within a month.

# TANDOORI SPICE MIX

There are many recipes for Tandoori spice mixtures online, but I have never seen one published that produces authentic restaurant results. This one does, although of course the results won't be exact without a tandoor oven, but the flavor here is actually authentic - and delicious.

| | |
|---|---|
| 1 t | Cumin Seeds |
| 1 t | Coriander Seeds |
| 1 t | Ginger, ground |
| 1 t | Turmeric |
| 1 t | Paprika |
| 3/4 t | Kashmiri Chili Powder or (not as good) Cayenne |
| 1/2 t | Cinnamon |
| 1/2 t | Garlic Powder |
| 1/2 t | Citric Acid |
| 6 | Cloves, whole (the spice, not garlic) |
| 1 T | Dark Brown Sugar |
| 2 t | Salt |

This is generally used as a paste by mixing it up with yogurt and ghee, as explained below. Alternatively the citric acid may be replaced with lemon juice, this adds more water to the mixture (lemon juice is mostly water) and the results will not be as professional.

## TANDOORI SPICE PASTE

Whisk together a ratio of 3 tablespoons of the Tandoori spice mix with 60 grams (2 ounces) of yogurt (not low-fat) and 30 grams (1 ounce) ghee or melted butter. Add red food coloring to suit yourself (restaurants add a lot). This is enough for four chicken quarters (marinate overnight). For short marinade times such as with shrimp, allow this mixture to stand at room temperature for at least an hour before you *start* the marinade process. For longer marinades, you can use it immediately. High temperature cooking is essential for the flavor. After roasting and broiling (or grilling), sprinkle with fresh lemon juice and minced cilantro.

## DRIED PLUM SPICE MIX

As I wrote in the introduction, one of my goals is to bring to light exotic and delicious flavors that are unfamiliar to most people. Here is a splendid example of that.

| | |
|---|---|
| 1 T | Dried Plums, ground (page 24) |
| 1 1/2 t | Celery Salt |
| 3/4 t | Bittersweet Paprika (page 23) |
| 3/4 t | MSG |
| 1/2 t | Cinnamon, ground |
| 1/2 t | Sugar, powdered |
| 1/8 t | Cayenne |
| 1/8 t | Cloves, ground |

If you can't get celery salt, use 1 teaspoon dried celery root or dried celery leaves and 1/2 teaspoon salt. It isn't quite as good, though. You can also substitute regular paprika for the bittersweet, but again the result will not be as good. Grind the ingredients together and store in a closed bottle.

## CENTRAL ASIAN SPICE MIX

I would call this Uzbeki Spice Mix, but it isn't strictly Uzbeki and it has more general applications.

| | |
|---|---|
| 1 T | Cumin Seeds |
| 1 T | Coriander Seeds |
| 2 1/2 t | Salt |
| 2-3 whole | Dried Red Serrano Chilies |
| 1/2 star | Star Anise |
| 1/2 t | MSG (optional) |
| 1/4 t | Nigella (black cumin seeds) |

Simply grind all of the ingredients together in an electric spice mill until a powder. Bottle and store in a cool, dark place. Ideally you should use it within a month, as the flavor diminishes on prolonged storage.

# SPICE MIXTURE FOR RACK OF LAMB

I used to use the Egyptian spice mixture Dukkah for racks of lamb, but over the years I made modifications to improve the results. You can see the origin in the list of ingredients here, but this mixture is more intense and distinctive.

| | |
|---|---|
| 2 T | Pistaschio nuts (shelled) |
| 2 t | Brown Sugar, ideally Muscovado |
| 3/4 t | Cumin Seeds |
| 3/4 t | Salt, coarse |
| 1/4 - 1/2 t | Black Peppercorns, whole |
| 1/2 t | Sumac |
| 1/2 t | Coriander Seeds |
| 1/2 t | MSG |
| 1/4 - 1/2 t | Cayenne |
| 1/4 t | Cinnamon, ground |

Adjust the quanity of black pepper and cayenne to suit your own preferences for spiciness. Score the fat cap of the lamb rack and then rub with olive oil before applying the spice mixture. Be generous with the spice. One of the main differences between home and restaurant cooking is the liberal use of seasonings. The amount shown here is about the amount used for a single rack of lamb in a restaurant - all of it!

Simply grind all of the ingredients together in an electric spice mill. They do not need to be ground to a powder, but make sure there are no large pieces left. Bottle and store in a cool, dark place. Like all spice blends, the sooner you use it after grinding, the better the taste will be. Ideally you should use it within a month, as the flavor diminishes on prolonged storage.

# SPACE FOR NOTES

# Killer Cocktails 2!

As you probably know from my videos on YouTube, I am the author of *Cocktails of the South Pacific and Beyond*. The cocktail recipes presented here were all developed after the publication of that book, so there are no duplicates.

## LA SERVA PADRONA

Named after an Italian opera by Gennaro Antonio Federico. The twisted tale is about a wealthy bachelor who is bossed around by his young maid. Through a convoluted scheme of deception, he gets the girl to agree to marry him because he loves being dominated by her.

Although it looks like a minor component in quanity, *Amaro Montenegro* is the soul of this cocktail. An amaro—and there are many—is an entire class of Italian bitter herbal liqueurs. This one is from Bologna and it has notes of vanilla and orange along with its complex herbal profile. Another example is *Amaro Nonino*.

Begin by putting 2 teaspoons of sugar on a saucer. Douse the sugar with about <u>10 drops of Angostura bitters</u> and mix it to form a ring that is about the same diameter as your intended glass. Rub the rim of a chilled glass goblet with fresh lime and then dip into the sugar/bitters. Combine:

| | |
|---|---|
| 45ml (1.5 oz) | Brandy, ideally Asbach Urlacht (German) |
| 30ml (1 oz) | Grand Marnier |
| 10ml (1/3 oz) | Amaro Montenegro (an Italian liqueur) |
| 30ml (1 oz) | Blood Orange Juice, fresh |
| 22ml (3/4 oz) | Lime Juice, fresh |

Shake with ice and strain into the glass. Add a maraschino cherry.

## BABAASH

The name is Trinidadian for a kind of native fruit rum that this was inspired by. I have provided a recipe for a Spiced Rum below, but it is even better with *The Kraken Black Spiced Rum* from Trinidad—if you can get it. Nicole Fortune, where are you?

| | |
|---|---|
| 30ml (1 oz) | Grapefruit Juice, fresh |
| 30ml (1 oz) | Cranberry Juice, ideally organic |
| 15ml (1/2 oz) | Spiced Rum (see note above) |
| 1 teaspoon | Cointreau |
| 6-8 drops | Rhubarb bitters, Fee Bros. (see note below) |

Shake with ice and strain into fluted glass. Add about:

| | |
|---|---|
| ~45ml (1 1/2 oz) | Champagne, brut (*e.g.* Piper-Heidsieck) |

Optional garnish: Balls of honeydew melon skewered on a swizzle stick. Put a tiny bit of fine sea salt on the melon.

If you are craving this drink and don't have champagne on hand, you can make a non-sparkling version with a good Chardonnay. You can also substitute Angostura bitters for the Rhubarb bitters and still have a fine cocktail.

## QUICKLY SPICED RUM

This can made on short notice and will produce a natural taste, unlike most inexpensive commercial "spiced rums".

| | |
|---|---|
| 60ml (2 oz) | Bacardi Black Rum |
| 3 | Allspice, whole |
| 3 | Cloves, whole |
| 1 segment | Star Anise (not a whole star) |
| 1 pod | Green Cardamom |
| 1 teaspoon | Vanilla Sugar (or dark brown sugar) |
| 1 strip | Orange Zest, no white pith |

Crush the spices in a mortar and put everything together in a jar with a screw lid. Shake occasionally over about 30 minutes. Strain through linen. For a more subtle version, use more rum and let it stand longer (*e.g.* quadruple the rum and let it sit for 1-2 days).

## TIGER CLAW

You'll never know what hit you. Begin by putting 2 teaspoons of sugar in an electric spice mill with <u>6 whole Allspice</u>. Grind, then pass through a fine mesh sieve. Discard spice that won't pass through the sieve. Rub the inside rim of a martini glass with a cut lemon and pour in the sugar/allspice. Roll the powder around and then shake out the excess. For making the pomegranate syrup, see my *Cocktails of the South Pacific* book.  Combine:

| | |
|---|---|
| 30ml (1 oz) | Vodka |
| 30ml (1 oz) | Apricot Brandy, Marie Brizzard |
| 30ml (1 oz) | Lemon Juice, fresh |
| 15ml (1/2 oz) | Pineapple Juice |
| 1 teaspoon | Pomegranate Syrup (or substitute Grenadine) |

Shake with ice and strain into the glass. Float:

| | |
|---|---|
| 1 teaspoon | 151-proof Rum, Bacardi (optional) |

A professional touch is to serve this in a tiger-print martini glass. There are some stunning designs available online.

## IPU-KULA

The Hawaiian name translates to *cup of gold*. This is an especially food-friendly cocktail, great for sipping with anything from roasted ham to chow mein.

| | |
|---|---|
| 30ml (1 oz) | Gold Rum |
| 30ml (1 oz) | Cachaça |
| 7.5 ml (1/4 oz) | Nocino (Italian walnut liqueur) |
| 30ml (1 oz) | Grapefruit Juice, fresh |
| 15ml (1/2 oz) | Apple Juice |
| 15ml (1/2 oz) | Lime Juice, fresh |
| 7.5 ml (1/4 oz) | Ginseng Syrup |

Shake with cracked ice and then strain into a chilled martini glass, or dump the entire mixture (with the ice) into a chilled brandy snifter. Add an orchid and a straw.

# AUNT DOVE

As the name suggests, this is a family recipe from my father's Aunt Dove. His entire family was involved in the bootlegging business during Prohibition, as I explained in my cocktail book. Aunt Dove was mostly known as a medium who would pretend to talk to the spirit world. She had many tricks for making noises and shining colored lights by remote controls that must have been very convincing on rubes in the 1920's, because she became wealthy enough to buy an entire city block of downtown Kansas City.

| | |
|---|---|
| 60ml (2 oz) | Vodka |
| 30ml (1 oz) | Spiced Cherry Whiskey (see recipe below) |
| 15ml (1/2 oz) | Peachtree Schnapps |
| 8-10 drops | Peach bitters (or Angostura - see note below) |

The "vodka" in this recipe and the bourbon in the spiced cherry below were both moonshine originally. Also, it was probably served at room temperature, I prefer it shaken with ice. You can substitute Angostura bitters with fairly good results, but the peach bitters make this a real treat. I suggest *The Bitter Truth* brand of peach bitters for this. Finally, if you can get moonshine, then all the better.

# SPICED CHERRY WHISKEY

Infusing flavors into liquor is an old art that was once a cornerstone of good bartending, although it is not done much these days. There are many more preparations like this in my book, *Cocktails of the South Pacific*, including authentic recipes dating back to the 1920's.

Put the following into a glass jar with a lid:

| | |
|---|---|
| 90ml (3 oz) | Bourbon Whiskey, such as Jim Beam |
| 80g (2.8 oz) | Sour Cherries, okay frozen (not sweet cherries) |
| 1 Tablespoon | Sugar, white |
| 1/2 teaspoon | Black Peppercorns |
| 1 whole | Star Anise |

Let it stand at room temperature for 18-24 hours, swirling occasionally. Pass through a sieve, and then through linen.

## BLACK BOMBAY

Black Elvis Rum and Dark Elvis Rum are from India—of all places! They do not qualify as true rums in my opinion, at least by the taste. However, they are delicious and extremely useful in cocktails, possessing a complex deep flavor with notes of bittersweet chocolate, caramel, tropical fruit and a hint of burnt orange. This cocktail plays on those natural flavors. If there is any justice in the liquor trade, these products will gain popularity in the future.

Also note that both lychee syrup and lychee liqueurs decompose. After a couple of years there is very little actual lychee flavor left.

| | |
|---|---|
| 60ml (2 oz) | Dark Elvis Rum, or Black Elvis Rum |
| 15ml (1/2 oz) | Creme de Cacao |
| 15ml (1/2 oz) | Lychee Liqueur, Bols |
| 1 teaspoon | Cointreau |
| 15ml (1/2 oz) | Lemon Juice, fresh |

Shake with ice and strain into a chilled martini glass.

## THE WETTER THE BETTER

This is a Dry Martini in full reverse...at maximum speed.

| | |
|---|---|
| 45ml (1 1/2 oz) | Gin or Vodka |
| 30ml (1 oz) | Dry Vermouth |
| 30ml (1 oz) | Dry White Wine (*e.g.* Oyster Bay Chardonnay) |
| 4-5 drops | Orange Bitters (optional) |

Stir with ice and strain into a chilled martini glass.

The original recipe of a Martini, which was a third vermouth, is all but forgotten. Over the decades the amount of vermouth has diminished until it practically disappeared out of the recipe completely. This very wet Martini has been especially well received in Russia where drinking straight chilled vermouth is popular.

While we're on the subject of Martini history, the drink James Bond was famous for is a Vesper, not a Martini. Also, "shaken not stirred" makes a Martini a Bradford (that's the only difference in the recipe).

# EVOLUTION

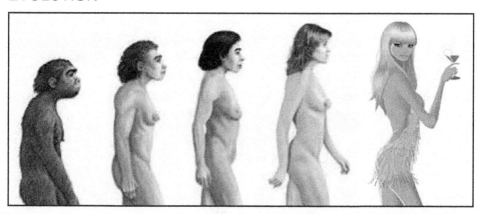

One of the female patrons who was fond of Martinis complained that she always felt like a man drinking one, and asked if she could have something similar but, "pink and more evolved".

| | |
|---|---|
| 60ml (2 oz) | Vodka |
| 30ml (1 oz) | Gin |
| 1 teaspoon | Creme de Noyeax (almond liqueur) |
| 1 teaspoon | Lemon Juice, fresh |
| 6-8 drops | Peychaud's bitters |

Shake with ice. Strain into a chilled martini glass.

# HORSERADISH VODKA

Infusing flavors into liquor is an old art that was once a hallmark of good bartenders. It is still very much alive in rural Russia.

| | |
|---|---|
| 15g (1/2 oz) | Horseradish, fresh (cut into slices) |
| 200ml (7 oz) | Vodka |

Put this in a jar in your refrigerator for 1-2 days, then remove the horseradish pieces and transfer the bottle to your freezer. Keep shot glasses in your freezer for serving this. It needs to be extremely cold to be at its best. Especially suited as an apertif before Beef Stroganoff.

## KAMA'AINA

Based on an old Trader Vic cocktail of the same name, but different from the recipe you usually see in print. Also, despite the restaurant's bar menu translating the name of this drink to "old timer" for at least the last half century, that's not a very accurate translation. The word is Hawaiian for anyone who has been living in Hawaii for a long time (not necessarily born there).

| | |
|---|---|
| 45ml (1 1/2 oz) | Gin, ideally Tanqueray |
| 30ml (3/4 oz) | Coconut Rum |
| 10ml (1/3 oz) | Cointreau |
| 15ml (1/2 oz) | Lemon Juice, fresh |
| 15ml (1/2 oz) | Lime Juice, fresh |
| 20ml (2/3 oz) | Cream, heavy |

Shake well with ice and then add:

| | |
|---|---|
| 60ml (2 oz) | 7-Up, or (better) Sprite |

Swirl carefully and then strain into a lowball glass. Add a spear with a pineapple slice and maraschino cherry.

## COCONUT CLUB COCKTAIL

Inspired by the Coconut Grove cocktail that just about every celebrity in Hollywood had imbibed in the 1930's. If you want to make this a real knockout drink, swap Kalani Coconut Liqueur in place of the Malibu Coconut Rum. Marie Brizzard's is also good.

| | |
|---|---|
| 75ml (2 1/2 oz) | Gin, ideally Plymouth |
| 10ml (1/3 oz) | Malibu Coconut Rum (see above) |
| 1 teaspoon | Maraschino Liqueur |
| 1 teaspoon | Lime Juice, fresh |
| 1/4 teaspoon | Powdered Sugar |

Combine all of the ingredients in a shaker with a lot of ice. Stir using a bar spoon for about 20 seconds. Strain into a small frozen martini glass. It should be frosty white. Garnish with a short thin ribbon of orange zest.

# AVENGER

Violet syrup can taste like a scented candle if it is not used judiciously. The Currant black balsam from Riga is the one in the black bottle with the purple and silver label. Don't confuse this with their regular balsam in the brown bottle. If you are substituting Creme d'Cassis then add another teaspoon or so of lime juice.

| | |
|---|---|
| 75ml (2 1/2 oz) | Vodka |
| 22ml (3/4 oz) | Riga *Currant* Black Balsam, or Creme d'Cassis |
| 1 teaspoon | Violet Syrup |
| 10ml (1/3 oz) | Lime Juice, fresh (see note above) |

Shake with ice and strain into a chilled martini glass, or on the rocks in a lowball glass.

If you like this drink, then you are sure to enjoy the Violet Liqueur made by *The Bitter Truth* (www.the-bitter-truth.com/liqueurs/creme-violette). This is just a tip and not a paid endorsement, by the way.

# A Few Final Words

**Note: In some cases small quantities of basic supplies such as vegetable oil, flour, water, sugar, salt and ground black pepper have not been specified in the list of ingredients in order to leave room for the more notes.**

**Whenever you are in doubt about something, consult the video. Don't forget to look through the comments section on that particular video, too. Many common questions have been left by viewers that I've already answered. Of course you can also ask your own questions anytime. I usually respond within a few hours.**

www.youtube.com/user/cookinginrussia

On this site you will find a short video
explaining how to search for my other video recipes.

# IN PRAISE OF OLDER MUSHROOMS

Champignons, also known as button mushrooms, begin to shrivel up and darken as they linger forlorn in the bottom of your refrigerator vegetable bin. Within a few days they can look like they are ready to be thrown out, which unfortunately is the fate that often befalls them. The truth is that these can be an incredible asset in your cooking if you know how to use them. Leaving mushrooms next to carrots and celery in a vegetable bin and allowing them to dry will intensify their flavor and give them a more leathery, meaty texture that can stand up to braises—as well as being ideal for poultry stuffing.

Two cautionary notes here, though. First, if the mushrooms actually begin to turn moldy (usually white fuzz or a slimy texture) then game over—you went too far. Also, this advice only applies to champignons. Most every other mushroom should either be cooked while fresh, or dried properly with the right equipment when it is still fresh.

The next time you find yourself with some forgotten button mushrooms that have shrunk to half their size and turned walnut brown, try rinsing them off and then cooking them up with some bacon and onion. Then add a little white wine and let them poach in it long and slow. Now you have a mixture that can be incorporated into a poultry stuffing (add cubes of dried bread and whole egg), or chopped up and used as a filling for omelettes, or baked with eggplant and Bechamel sauce, etc. The possibilities are vast, and once you taste the result, you might start *purposely* leaving mushrooms in the bottom of your fridge to dry up from then on.

# CARAMELIZING VS. BROWNING ONIONS

One of the tricks that I have used in several of my videos is the addition of a catalytic quantity of baking soda to onions when they are cooking to accelerate the Maillard reaction. It is important to realize that onions that are "browned" in this manner are not the same as onions slowly caramelized by the traditional method (or onions that have been braised, as in my *French Onion Soup* video). If you search online, you'll find this baking soda "trick" is now widely known, but it seems no one is aware that the end product is distinctly different from slowly cooked onions. Furthermore, adding either vinegar or lemon juice to the finished product to remove the excess alkaline baking soda seems to be a step these other people never learned about. The human palate doesn't like alkaline tastes, so baking soda (or anything else alkaline) should always be neutralized for the best flavor.

There is also an important distinction between caramelizing and browning foods, particularly in the case of onions. Many times you find these two words used interchangeably, but technically they are not at all the same. While caramelized onions do turn brown (of course), actual "browned onions" are cooked at a high heat so that the outside darkens while the inside is still soft and white. This produces a different flavor profile from either slow caramelization or the baking-soda enhanced Maillard reaction type of cooked onions.

You can think of these three types in terms of how sweet or how savory you want the onion to be. The most sweet is the type cooked with baking soda. The most savory are onions cooked at a high temperature—and the more you go in that direction, the more savory they become, such as in my *Uzbeki Plov* recipe (page 66). Falling somewhere in between these two extremes are onions that have been caramelized slowly without any baking soda.

# A Dozen Food Myths

## RAW EGGS AND SALMONELLA

The fear of salmonella has almost eliminated one of the most useful ingredients in cooking. Namely, raw eggs. There are three things to consider here:

1. The contimination is nearly always on the outside shell of the egg. Washing eggs well with warm soapy water will kill over 99% of salmonella. Of course this won't affect the inside, but...

2. Salmonella inside an egg is very rare. The CDC estimates that only one egg in 20,000 is internally contaminated. If you ate a raw egg every day, 365 days a year, statistically you would not encounter Salmonella for 54 years (as long as you washed them first).

3. Eggs got a bad reputation as carriers of Salmonella because of an epidemic outbreak in the 1980's that was traced to infected henhouses. Steps were taken to correct that problem. The fact is that Salmonella can be present on fruit, especially melons. So shall we cook melons now to be safe?

Have you made your own mayonnaise? Made your own ice cream? Have you eaten cookie dough? Those things contain raw eggs. Technically speaking, eating raw eggs is a risk, but if you are a healthy adult it should not be a serious concern.

Disclaimer: For pregnant women, children under 5, the elderly and those with a compromised immune system, it's best to be paranoid (legally speaking).

# VINEGAR DAMAGES YOUR STOMACH

This fear is especially prevalent in Russia. There are two reasons for this. First, Russians seem to be genetically predisposed to stomach disorders. Coupled with a long history of very simple foods, a wide range of folklore about foods developed that are often completely wrong. For instance, many believe that all soups are bad for you, and forbidden if you have stomach problems. The fact is that as long as it's reasonably low in fat and sodium, soup is one of the best things you can eat if you have stomach problems.

The belief that vinegar burns your stomach is prevalent in many nations, but especially Russia. It seems justified on the surface, because vinegar is acidic to the taste. The problem with this notion is that your stomach is over 100 times more acidic than vinegar. It can't burn your stomach any more than one ice cube can cool down a bathtub of water. Russians are sensitive to anything acidic because there are no sour foods in the cuisine.

# SALT IS BAD FOR YOU

For decades the conventional wisdom by the medical profession has been that we all eat too much salt. The FDA set the health guideline for salt intake to 2,300mg a day as a maximum. The fact is that the jury is still out on this—and in a very big way.

First, recent studies have suggested that we may not be eating *enough* salt, believe it or not. A *minimum* intake of 3,000mg a day has been suggested—that's more than the previous maximum was! This same study says 6,000mg should be the new maximum. For more about this, point your browser to:

http://tinyurl.com/eatmoresalt

Second, a discovery has been made that some people are "salt resistant", meaning that they have a genetic phenotype that allows them to eat very high amounts of salt without having high blood pressure, even when they are obese. I couldn't find a reference on the exact percentage of the population with this phenotype, but the studies imply that it is fairly common.

# Nine More Food Myths

1. **Cold tap water comes to a boil faster than hot water.**
I've encountered this myth in every country I've been in. It is
amazing how many people believe it. Just think about how
illogical this is. Obviously the cold water will take some time to
get as hot as the hot water you could have started with.

2. **Mushrooms should never be washed**—or if you are a fan
of Alton Brown's "Good Eats" series, then the myth is that
mushrooms should *always* be washed. Alton "proved this" by
weighing mushrooms before and after rinsing—even soaking—
them in water, to show the weight was unchanged. The problem
with his experiment is that he only tried that with one specific
type of mushroom. Champignons (also known as button
mushrooms) are dense and not very absorbant. Feel free to
wash those as much as you like. Just don't think about doing
that with morels or any other mushroom that is porous. You are
not only washing away tons of flavor, but you are making sure
that the mushroom will not cook properly.

3. **Italians never combine fish and cheese.** People just like
to simplify everything because it's easier to remember. General
trends get made into hard and fast rules that are rarely accurate.
This is certainly one of them. First of all, the presence of
anchovies does not count as fish in a dish. Anchovies are
frequently added in tiny portions for umami and depth of flavor,
but not so the dish has a profoundly fishy taste. Parmesan and
anchovies are perfectly normal partners. Second—and I can't
stress this enough—regional variations. What is unthinkable
culinary blasphemy in one part of Italy almost always has some
counterpart in another region where the very same combination
is part of their proud local heritage. There are plenty of Italian
dishes with fish and all sorts of cheeses. They just didn't

become internationally famous, so this overstated rule of "no fish and cheese" has managed to survive intact.

4. **Don't add oil to pasta water**. Once again we have Alton Brown to thank for this myth. Although he did partially apologize in a later episode, still, he only gets partial credit because he missed two of the three reasons for doing this. A little olive oil in water that pasta is cooking helps reduce frothing (he admitted that later). What Alton didn't seem to learn in chemistry class is that the solubility of oil in water increases with temperature. So, just because the oil floats on the surface of cold water, that has nothing to do with how it behaves at a boil. Olive oil perfumes the pasta slightly with and also coats the pasta slightly to help prevent it from sticking to itself. Alton is generally a great source of information, but he's not a scientist by any stretch of the imagination. I'm tempted to say more but I'll spare him because he has done *far, far* more good than harm.

5. **Wash your hands with the hottest water you can stand**. The idea is that this will kill more bacteria than luke warm water. The first problem with this idea is that bacteria are better at surviving in hot water than your skin cells are. Soap is what kills the bacteria, not hot water. Now, when it comes to washing grease off, hot water is the way to go. Don't use anti-bacterial soap, either. That actually makes things worse in the long run.

6. **Bread in meat is just cheap filler, or extender**. This is an especially pervasive myth among Americans who are used to seeing advertising that proclaims 100% beef. Bread, rice or some other starch is a necessity for tenderness, as well as acting as a sponge to retain fat and moisture. In Italy it is common to use 40% bread in meatballs. If you want intense meat flavor, then use demi glace to moisten your bread crumbs. The toughest meatballs you can make are from pure meat that has been kneaded extensively, so go easy on the mixing, too.

7. **There's no point in weighing packaged ingredients**. Just because a package states that it contains a certain weight of product doesn't mean you should trust that figure. This is especially true in restaurants where small individual errors can add up to a huge miscalculation when combining dozens of packages for a recipe. Having traveled around quite a lot and weighed thousands of products in different countries, I can tell you that American products virtually always contain more than the amount stated, sometimes by as much as 10%. Russian products always contain less than the package states, sometimes by as much as 10%. Italian products are all over the map, sometimes less and sometimes more. German products rarely deviate by more than 0.1%—but weigh everything anyway.

8. **Don't put pepper or spices on meat that will be browned because they will burn**. This is true if you are browning your meat over an open fire. Otherwise the moisture on the surface of the meat—as well as the fat you are browning the meat in—protects spices from turning into charcoal. The temperature that black pepper burns at is 162°C (325°F), which is well above the boiling point of water—so as long as there is steam coming off of the meat, there is no chance of burning. Foods being deep fried are generally protected by steam, too.

9. **MSG is bad for you**. I addressed this urban legend in Volume 1. The Internet is an ocean of fear mongering and misinformation. Usually for profit (asking for donations). The MSG myth is jokingly known among food scientists as *Chinese Restaurant Syndrome*. It is a psychosomatic disorder with absolutely no basis in logic or any credible evidence. Your own body produces about 60 grams (over 2 ounces) of glutamate per day. Without it, you would literally die. Virtually every food you eat contains some MSG because sodium ions are abundant and glutamate is one of the fundamental amino acids that make up proteins.

Average MSG found naturally present in foods (grams per kilogram)

| Food Item | Glutamate | MSG |
|-----------|-----------|-----|
| Human Breast Milk | 0.22 | 0.26 |
| Eggs | 0.23 | 0.27 |
| Beef | 0.33 | 0.38 |
| Chicken | 0.44 | 0.51 |
| Potatoes | 1.02 | 1.18 |
| Corn | 1.30 | 1.51 |
| Oysters | 1.37 | 1.59 |
| Broccoli | 1.76 | 2.04 |
| Mushrooms | 1.80 | 2.09 |
| Peas | 2.00 | 2.32 |
| Grape Juice | 2.58 | 2.99 |
| Tomato Juice | 2.60 | 3.02 |
| Tomato Purée (Pasata) | 4.56 | 5.29 |
| Tuna, canned | 6.00 | 6.96 |
| Walnuts | 6.58 | 7.63 |
| Soy Sauce | 10.90 | 12.64 |
| Parmesan Cheese | 12.00 | 13.92 |
| Roquefort Cheese | 12.80 | 14.85 |

## The weight of 1 teaspoon of pure MSG = 1.62 grams

The first numeric column in the table above is the pure glutamate, as published by the American Chemical Society. However, we can't compare those figures to MSG directly because the molecular weight of glutamate does not include the sodium ion. The column on the right is the corrected weight.

**To put this in perspective, a recipe that calls for half a teaspoon of MSG for four servings contains the same amount of MSG as 1 1/4 teaspoons of soy sauce, or 37 grams (1.3 oz) of tomato purée, or about 8 mushrooms, or 15 grams (a half ounce) of Parmesan cheese per serving.**

✦

# Recipe Index

## A

## B

## C

## D

*225*

## P

Pancakes, 54
Parsnips (Deep Fried), 158
Pasta alla Puttanesca, 94
Planka (Swedish), 164
Pork (or Goat) Methi, 154
Port Wine Barbecue Sauce, 134
Potatoes from Dopplebock Beef, 116

## R

Roasted Pork (Korean Style), 104
Russian Tuna Salad Sandwich, 180

## S

Salmon Curry, 98
Sausage and Potatoes, 62
Shrimp with Mushrooms in a Wine and Cream Sauce, 76
Smoked Clam Chowder with Celery Root and Scotch Whisky, 110
Sonora Madelines, 84
Spaghetti Carbonara with Smoky Egg Yolk, 160
Spice Mixture for Rack of Lamb, 201
Spiced Beef and Artichoke Wrap, 178
Spicy Korean BBQ Sauce, 150
Starlight Meatballs, 130
Steak au Poivre, 140
Swedish Planka, 164

## T

Tandoori Spice Mix and Paste, 199
Tapas Grilled Cheese Sandwich, 174
Thai Duck and Pineapple Curry, 102
Tochitură, 148

## U

Uzbeki Plov, 66

## V

Venezuelan Blackened Chicken, 80

CPSIA information can be obtained at www.ICGtesting.com
Printed in the USA
BVOW08s0305150716

455408BV00003B/167/P